Also by Richard H. Underwood
Gaslight Lawyers: Criminal Trials & Exploits in Gilded Age New York
CrimeSong: True Crime Stories from Southern Murder Ballads

SPRINGTIME
for SOPHIE

Courtroom Scene: Trial of Sophia Kritchman and Joe Mitchell, 1910.
Unknown photographer. (1)

RICHARD H. UNDERWOOD

SPRINGTIME *for* SOPHIE

MURDER AND MADNESS IN A CONNECTICUT MILL TOWN

Shadelandhouse
MODERN PRESS

Lexington, Kentucky

A Shadelandhouse Modern Press book

Springtime for Sophie
Murder and Madness in a Connecticut Mill Town

Shadelandhouse, Shadelandhouse Modern Press, and the colophon are trademarks
of Shadelandhouse Modern Press, LLC.

For information about permission to reproduce selections from this book,
please email permissions@smpbooks.com or direct inquiries to:
Permissions, Shadelandhouse Modern Press, LLC,
P.O. Box 910913, Lexington, KY 40591

Published in the United States by
Shadelandhouse Modern Press, LLC
Lexington, Kentucky
smpbooks.com
First edition 2025

Library of Congress Control Number: 2025943512
ISBN: 978-1-945049-00-2 (paperback)
ISBN: 978-1-945049-63-7 (epub)

The lines quoted on page xiii are from Margaret Atwood, *Alias Grace*, p. 23
(Nan A. Talese, an imprint of Double Day, 1996) and are used with permission.

Printed and manufactured in the United States of America
Book design and page layout: iota books
Cover design: Matt Tanner
Cover art: Annelisa Hermosilla, *Sophie*, pen and ink on art paper, 8 x 10
inches, (2021). Based on a black and white photograph in the public domain,
1910 (unknown photographer).

For Ethan

Geoffrey of Hougham appeals Godard of Witham and Humphrey his brother for slaying Robert, [Geoffrey's] son; and this he offers to prove as one who is past [fighting] age and as of his own sight and hearing, if the court shall consider that he may deraign it. And the king's sergeant and the two knights who made view of the wounded man (who lived four weeks and a half after the wounding), testify that Robert said that Godard and Humphrey thus wounded him, and that should he get well, he would deraign this against them, and should he not, then he wished that his death might be imputed to them. And the jurors of the wapentake of Wraggoe where he was slain, on being asked, said that they suspect them of the said death. Afterwards came Geoffrey and withdrew himself and put himself in mercy. His amercement is one mark, for which Robert of Rasen is pledge.

—F.W. Maitland (ed.), I *Select Pleas of the Crown No. 27*
Lincolnshire Eyre, A.D. 1202
(Selden Society, 1888)

[Earl of] Salisbury: May this be possible? May this be true?

Melun [a French lord]: Have I not hideous death within my view,

Retaining but a quantity of life,

Which bleeds away even as a form of wax

Resolveth from his figure 'gainst the fire?

What in the world should make me now deceive,

Since I must lose the use of all deceit?

Why should I then be false, since it is true

That I must die here and live hence by truth?

—Shakespeare, *King John*, V.iv.21–29

Sometimes at night I whisper it over to myself:
Murderess, Murderess. It rustles, like a taffeta skirt across the floor.
Murderer is merely brutal. It's like a hammer, or a lump of metal.
I would rather be a murderess than a murderer, if those are the only choices.

—Margaret Atwood, *Alias Grace*

CONTENTS

For murther, though it have no tongue, will speak
With most miraculous organ.

—Shakespeare, *Hamlet*, II.ii.593-594

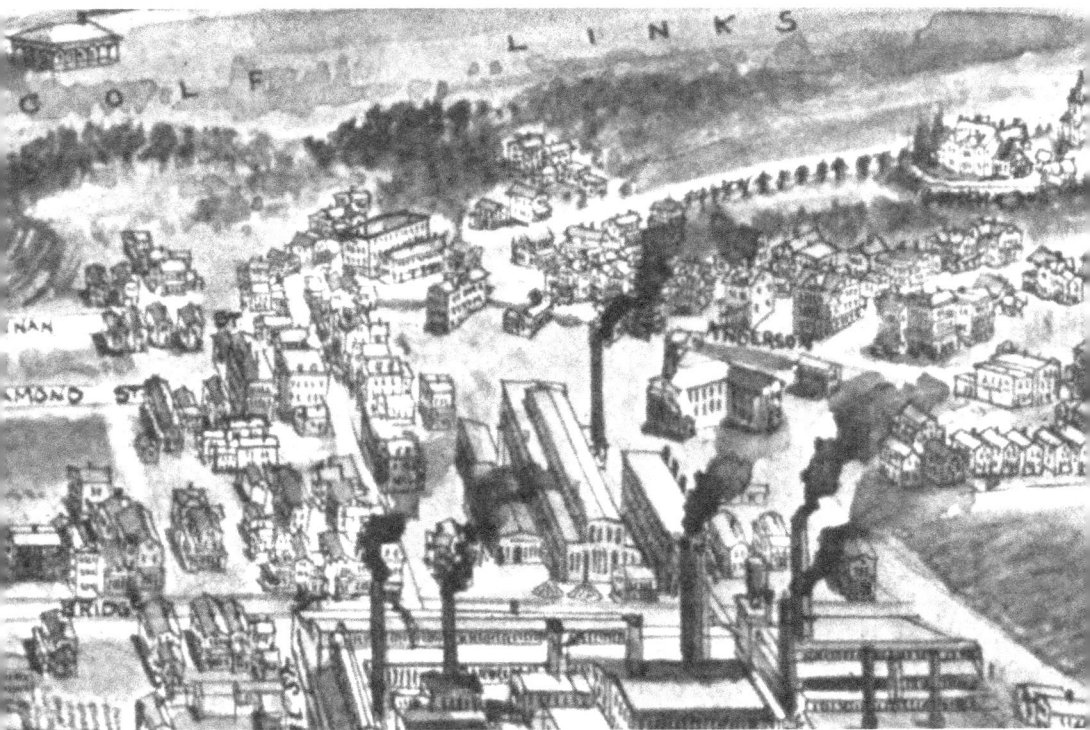

Detail from Bird's-eye view of Naugatuck, Connecticut, 1906,
Hughes & Bailey (2)

PREFACE

Nemo moriturus praesumitur mentire.
(A dying person is not presumed to lie.)

Imagine a lovers' triangle. A man and a woman are charged with luring another man to a remote location and killing him. The woman later tries, as best she can, to lay responsibility for the murder on her alleged partner in crime. She gets a lighter sentence as a reward for her act of betrayal.

This is not exactly an unusual scenario. In fact, I wrote of a similar case, the *Nack-Thorn-Guldensuppe* case, in a 2007 law review article,[1] which I later incorporated into *Gaslight Lawyers: Criminal Trials & Exploits in Gilded Age New York*, a nonfiction book about a gallery of notable lawyers in the Gaslight Era, also known as the Second Golden Age of the New York Bar, and their late nineteenth and early twentieth century New York City murder trials.[2] It also reminds me of an even earlier case involving a love triangle, the Tom Dula (Dooley) murder of Laura Foster, probably committed with the assistance of Ann Melton. That was a one-man, two-woman triangle. Tom was hanged, and Laura escaped punishment. I dissected the case in my nonfiction book *CrimeSong: True Crime Stories from Southern Murder Ballads*, which deals with historic stories of true crimes behind more than twenty such ballads.[3]

I thought the *Nack-Thorn-Guldensuppe* case was extraordinary until I ran across a 2009 retrospective in the *New York Daily News* while I was looking for materials about the dying declaration exception to the hearsay rule for my class in evidence law at the University of Kentucky J. David Rosenberg College of Law.[4] The article was about a long-forgotten murder in Waterbury, Connecticut, reported as *State of Connecticut v.*

Joseph Pecciulis, (alias Joseph Mitchell), and Sophie Kritchman.[5] The case was quite the sensation in its day.[6] The murder victim, Bronick (or Bronislaw or Bronislow) "Ben" Kulvinskas, had suffered twelve bullet wounds and had had his throat cut from ear to ear. Still, before he died, he named his killers, Sophia "Sophie" and Joseph "Joe," and his accusations made *in extremis* were admitted into evidence against them. As for the supposed partners in crime, in 1910 Sophie got a sentence of twelve to fifteen years for manslaughter, and poor Joe got life for second-degree murder. He was pardoned in 1923 when a case was made that he might have been convicted on "twisted" and perjured testimony.

As I researched the case, it became clear that there must have been doubts about Joe Mitchell's guilt almost from the start. At least the folks at the local newspaper were unconvinced of it. Keeping in mind that Joe was locked up from 1910 until 1923, consider the following excerpt from Volume I of *The History of Waterbury and the Naugatuck Valley*,[7] which was published in 1918 by William Jamieson Pape, the editor of the *Waterbury Republican*:

> On September 20, 1909, occurred the murder at Union City of Stanislaus [Ben] Kulvinskas. In this case, one of the most harrowing on record, the detective department worked up the evidence to the minutest detail, showing how the woman in the case, Sophie Kritchman, had first shot the man, then allowed him to lie dying in the woods for twenty-four hours. She then went back and cut the man's throat with a razor. When she found out later that he was still alive, she again shot him five times and left him dead as she thought. He was still breathing when discovered and died in a Waterbury hospital. The case first ended in a mistrial. Later, on a change of venue, she was convicted together with her lover, Joe Mitchell; *although the latter had no part in the actual murder* [emphasis added] he was given a life sentence and the woman was sent up for from twelve to fourteen [sic] years.

The story of Mitchell's hardship inspired William Thomas Walsh, a former reporter for the *Waterbury Republican*, noted historian, and

"Catholic author,"[8] to write a novel titled *Out of the Whirlwind* (1935). He told his readers that it was loosely based on an actual murder case, a *roman à clef* of sorts. An author's note says that he "made no effort to relate, save for the barest outline, the story of the actual crime and its consequences which suggested the plot to [him]." Still, the attention to detail from the actual case is striking.[9] Was he a reporter on the case? Was he related to the "Thomas W. Walsh" whom the newspaper described as a "court reporter" (rather than a newspaper reporter) who transcribed a detailed question-and-answer (Q&A) statement (later known as the Walsh Transcript) that Ben made about what had happened to him?

The novel goes on a bit too much about what was supposedly going on in the actors' minds and delves deeply into theology[10] (the title comes from the Book of Job).[11] *Out of the Whirlwind* drags on for 479 pages.[12] *Kirkus Reviews* observed that "an adequate sermon was preached" with religious "conversion as the high point."[13] The author of the review did not predict "a general sale for [the] book because it straddled its market too evidently."[14] Raymond Charles Krank, a reviewer writing in *The Brooklyn Citizen*, was a bit more mocking.

> The book is one long sermon. It traces a staggered path along the broad highway of Hell, through the burning track of Purgatory, and between the golden gates of Paradise, accompanied by a strange medley arrangement of "Life Is Just a Bowl of Cherries" and "*Te Deum*."[15]

One suspects that author Walsh would not have been happy with the review and may have thought that the acerbic Krank had been aptly named. I will have more to say about the novel in the afterword.

Two of the quotations I have set out in the front matter of this book illustrate that under British and American law dying declarations have long been admitted into evidence[16] under a hearsay exception (*hearsay* being out-of-court statements offered for the truth of the matter stated therein, which were not subject to cross-examination). How reliable is a dying declaration, given that the declarant may have been close to *delusional* because of his medical condition, *may not have had personal knowledge* of who inflicted his injuries and may have made unwarranted assumptions, and *may have had words put into his mouth* by the police or other interested persons?

One cannot confront and cross-examine a dead declarant to emphasize sources of unreliability—unless, of course, the victim survives and is available as a witness at trial, in which case the exception does not apply and is not needed.[17] The battle over reliability was fought out in the *Kritchman* case, but the defense counsel's challenges to Ben's (the victim's) supposed statements were unavailing.

Despite these obvious concerns, the reader might be surprised to learn how often dying declarations are used at trial—and even more surprised by the strange procedures that have been used to secure them. There have been several recent cases in which police have solicited throat-clicking noises or eye blinking as coded statements made by victims whose wounds left them unable to speak.[18]

Recently, legal commentators have raised the question of whether the dying declaration exception to the hearsay rule can survive the United States Supreme Court's new Confrontation Clause jurisprudence.[19] Perhaps that question will be answered before my little book sees the light of day.

The *Kritchman* case also presents a rather striking example of how an innocent person might be convicted as a result of *perjury* by a codefendant or other witnesses, *unreliable eyewitness identification* testimony, prosecutorial and police *misconduct*, and the *difficulties a defendant has in presenting a credible alibi*. These are serious problems to this day.[20] Another factor in the *Kritchman* case was almost certainly sympathy favoring Sophie, the female defendant.[21] The verdict was something of an odd compromise. The facts cried out for a conviction of someone for first-degree murder, and the verdict of manslaughter for Sophie seems hard to justify. Indeed, one of the few references to the *Kritchman* case that I have found was a very short account provided in Professor Lawrence B. Goodheart's book about capital punishment in Connecticut,[22] in which he accounts for Sophie's escape from the noose by her lawyer's focus on a male accomplice and on Sophie's entanglement in a "lethal sexual affair."[23] He put it this way:

The decision reflected ambiguity about who did what that undermined a first-degree murder conviction for either party. Kritchman's claim that she was coerced by a dominant male fit the norm of female passivity and male aggression. In that vein, a reporter described her as 'the young and pretty music teacher of Naugatuck,' not the stereotype of a heinous murderer.[24]

This is not a work of fiction. The story I am telling is bare bones, grounded in newspaper copy and in the limited number of surviving court documents. Indeed, what I have tried to do is reassemble the newspaper copy to tell a coherent story—to reorder witness accounts and reporters' observations. Even the title of the book comes from a newspaper story written at the time of Sophie's release from prison.

If this were a work of fiction, I could fill in gaps and inconsistencies, put words into the characters' mouths, and pretend to relate what they were thinking as the story unfolded. I could try to supply some explanation for what happened—some motive for the murder. At the 2014 Key West Literary Seminar, author and attorney Scott Turow observed (I am paraphrasing) that readers of crime fiction want explanations so that they do not feel they will be engulfed in random crime in real life. I suppose that this is a variation on the theme that truth is stranger than fiction, because fiction must be plausible.

One can speculate that Sophie Kritchman was paranoid and somewhat delusional. One can speculate that she had been a victim in her own right—perhaps a victim of rape or abuse. I can offer nothing else to explain this savage crime. This is what makes the story so chilling. I should also note that although her codefendant Joe Mitchell might very well have been acquitted if he had been tried separately, I cannot declare with any sense of certainty that he was innocent, even though, in the end, that seems to have been the verdict of the community.

Richard H. Underwood
Lexington, Kentucky
2025

Waterbury ("Brass City") and Naugatuck

Being a Midwesterner transplanted to Kentucky, I was prepared to believe that all towns in New England must be idyllic. However, I learned that Waterbury, Connecticut, the venue for one of the two trials of Sophie Kritchman (the second trial was moved to New Haven), was an industrial town known as "Brass City" for its importance in the manufacture of brass. It would "become a leader in the Industrial Revolution."[25] Indeed, the city motto is *Quid Aere Perennius*, which, for those of you who were not subjected to Latin in high school, means something like, "What is more lasting than brass?" Like other industrial towns of the period, Waterbury drew in many immigrant workers.

Waterbury, Connecticut, is in northern New Haven County on the Naugatuck River. Just a bit south is the town of Naugatuck, which consists of Union City on the east side of the Naugatuck River, Straitsville on the southeast, and Milleville on the west side of the river. Naugatuck, too, was a mill town that produced rubber, and Union City (part of Naugatuck—not a separate town) was the childhood home of Charles Goodyear. The Union City area that figures into our story was ethnically the Polish and Lithuanian section of Naugatuck served by the Catholic church of St. Hedwig Parish, founded in 1906.

Waterbury and Naugatuck are less than one hundred miles from Manhattan. In my mind I picture commuters going to New York City from Waterbury and back again on the train. In William Thomas Walsh's novel, *Out of the Whirlwind*, Waterbury, Naugatuck, and Union City are blended and given the unfortunate name of Hookerstown.

As a native of Columbus, Ohio, I was delighted to be reminded that Waterbury was the venue for Columbus native James Thurber's short story

Goodyear Metallic Rubber Shoe Company & Downtown Naugatuck,
Connecticut (circa 1890) (3)

"The Secret Life of Walter Mitty." Arthur Miller's salesman Willy Loman
might have passed through the area when he was riding his circuit. I was
also touched by the fact that the Waterbury Clock Company was saved
from bankruptcy in 1933 by sales of its Mickey Mouse watch. That would
have made a great holiday movie starring Jimmy Stewart.

Waterbury saw its share of controversy over the years. One of the first
birth control clinics in the country was sponsored by the daughters of
Henry Sabin Chase,[26] an industrialist who founded the Chase Brass &
Copper Company. This caused quite a ruckus in the heavily Catholic
town, because 1879 legislation criminalized the distribution of contracep-
tives. The law was struck down by the United States Supreme Court in
1965 in *Griswold v. Connecticut*, the famous "right to privacy" case.

And yes, every town's history has a dark side. In 1939 Waterbury
Mayor T. Frank Hayes was convicted of involvement in a conspiracy to
cheat and defraud the city out of more than one million dollars. He was
released from prison in 1949, and he died at age eighty-one.

If that was not bad enough, Waterbury resident George Metesky, the
"Mad Bomber," terrorized New York City from 1940 to 1956, taking a

Main Street from Union Street, Union City, Connecticut,
The August Schmelzer Co., Meriden, Connecticut (4)

patriotic sabbatical during World War II.[27] He was finally run to ground by an early profiler named Dr. James Brussel, who would later play a part in the "Boston Strangler" case.[28] It is reported that Metesky lived a quiet life in Waterbury after his release from an asylum, hanging out at the town library until his death in 1994 at age ninety. I wonder how many Waterbury moms had any idea that was going on when they dropped their kids off at the library.

Perhaps the reader remembers Waterbury native Bob Crane of *Hogan's Heroes*, whose lifestyle and death shocked and surprised many.

Then there was music teacher Sophie Kritchman, whose 1909–1910 murder trials are the subject of our story. It was not the first *love-inspired* crime of violence tried in Waterbury, according to the book *Wicked Waterbury: Madmen & Mayhem in the Brass City*, by Edith Reynolds and John Murray.[29] Indeed, one of the front-page news stories about the *Kritchman* case includes this lovely report of an unrelated murder:

Factory of The Waterbury Clock Company, Waterbury, 1893 (5)

HUSBAND HELD
FOR MURDER
OF HIS WIFE
Body Bound to Top of Gas
Stove and Then Burned
To Crisp[30]

The *Kritchman* case would get top billing even with this kind of competition. That neither of these stories made it into *Wicked Waterbury* came as something of a surprise to me. Perhaps the authors wanted to keep a wall between Waterbury and its neighbor to the south.

Sophie and Friends

Sophia Kritchman lived in a house on Anderson Street in Union City, if I have located the correct piece of property. It had been built in 1900 and was owned by her mother. The house can be spotted on a 1906 map of Naugatuck (detail), illustration 2 of this book. Anderson Street runs off of Spring Street, and Spring Street runs north toward Waterbury proper.

To the newspaper reporters, Sophie gave her age as eighteen. However, the Naugatuck Town Clerk's records would prove that she was born on October 11, 1885, which would have made her twenty-four at the time

Kritchman house (6)

Sophia [Sophie] Kritchman, circa 1910 (7)

of her first trial.[31] She was said to be "the pride of her family," and she was described as having had many advantages compared to other girls in the mill towns. At one time she had been employed in one of the local rubber factories, and she also worked for a while in a confectionery store. She was given schooling, and although she might not have been a star student, she did have a talent for music. Prior to murder, she had been devoting all her time to teaching music. Sophie had several pupils whom she tutored on the piano. She and her students had performed several concerts in Union City. Her many acquaintances thought she always displayed a "genial disposition."[32]

The reporters gave her mixed reviews on her looks. As the case proceeded, she was described as "pretty," but an earlier report noted that she was "pretty" but "could never be clast [sic] as an attractive girl." She had "many admirers among the Lithuanians" in her community. Still, it was said that she was "vain and frivolous in manner."[33]

Bronick (or Bronislaw or Bronislow) "Ben" Kulvinskas and his brother Antone (or Anton or Anthony) were boarders at the Kritchman

Bronislow Kulvinskas, The Murdered Man, circa 1910 (8)

Joseph Mitchell, Alleged Accomplice of Sophia [Sophie] Kritchman, 1910 (9)

home on Anderson Street. Testimony at the Kritchman trials related that the brothers had rooms on the second floor where Sophie also had a room.[34] Ben owned a saloon known as Kulvinskas Brothers, which was located at the corner of Anderson and School streets, not far from the Kritchman home. People assumed that Ben had money, as a business owner, and Sophie's parents encouraged her to be friendly to him. She would later testify that he tutored her in the Lithuanian language of her parents. Her knowledge of Lithuanian would prove to be of advantage later in her trials.[35]

Apparently Sophie had exhibited some affection for Ben. Both were interested in music, and he would accompany her piano playing on his trombone.[36] Despite the tie to Ben, it was said that Sophie favored Joe Mitchell, who was twenty-six and the younger and better-looking of the two suitors. Mitchell worked in the employ of others as a bartender. He lived in a room over the Mazikas & Pavolinis saloon on North Riverside Street.[37]

It would be conceded by Mitchell's counsel that Sophie and Mitchell had been sexually intimate.[38] She may have been intimate with Ben, too. It was established that Ben had urged Sophie to be his wife.[39]

PART ONE

As Ben Lay Dying

The Scene of the Crime

Around noon on Saturday, September 18, 1909, Bronick (or Bronislaw or Bronislow) "Ben" Kulvinskas was found at the Shady Nook ("the Nook"), also referred to as Lovers' Lane, a secluded spot on the Waterbury side of the Waterbury-Naugatuck line.

Several boys had passed close by the Nook, and Ben had called out to them for water. The frightened boys ran away and sought the assistance of Walter H. Roberts, who lived nearby.[40] Roberts went to the scene, and the following conversation took place between Roberts and Ben:

Roberts: "What is the matter with you?"
Kulvinskas: "I am shot, get a doctor, I am dying."
Roberts: "Do you know who shot you?"
Kulvinskas: "I do."
Roberts: "Who?"
Kulvinskas: "A Waterbury fellow and a Union City girl."
Roberts: "Where are you shot?"
Kulvinskas: "All over."
Roberts: "How many times were you shot?"
Kulvinskas: "About fifteen."[41]

Ben was covered with blood and close to death as a result of twelve bullet wounds[42] and a gash in his neck from ear to ear, two inches deep, and running in an upward direction. There were two bullet wounds in each of his hands, suggesting defense wounds.[43] There was one bullet wound at the base of his skull which had lacerated his brain, one in front of the right shoulder joint, one under the arm pit, one in the right ribs,

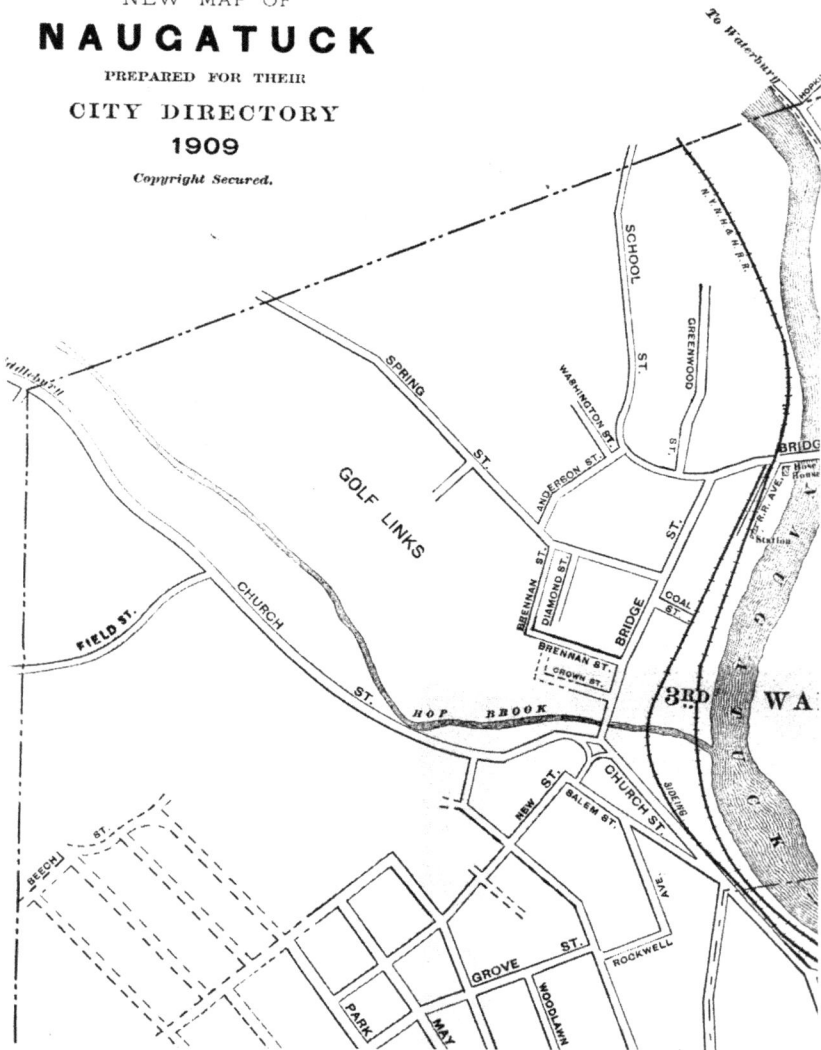

THE PRICE & LEE CO'S
NEW MAP OF
NAUGATUCK
PREPARED FOR THEIR
CITY DIRECTORY
1909
Copyright Secured.

A map of Naugatuck prepared by the Price & Lee Company for the 1909 city directory shows Anderson and Spring streets and the Golf Links, as well as the Naugatuck-Waterbury Line. (10)

"The Shady Nook in Lovers Lane," scene of Kulvinskas Murder, 1910,
Capt. Thomas Dodds, photographer (11)

and four in the abdomen. Bullet tracks went through the lower part of
his right lung and through his diaphragm and liver.

Ben lay dying between a wire fence and the bushes alongside an old,
grass-covered lane called the New England Road (presumably the railroad
bed where the old New England Railroad line had run). This old "road"
had been part of a "public highway" that had run from Naugatuck to the
old passenger station for the New York and New England Railroad.[44] A
map from a City Directory of Naugatuck dated 1909 shows Anderson
and Spring streets and the Golf Links (now Hop Brook Golf Course), as
well as the Naugatuck-Waterbury Line. Spring Street and the Golf Links,
which figure in the story, and the Kritchman house on Anderson, can
also be identified on illustration 2.

Police Chief John R. Schmidt was called to the scene, but he then
left to summon the medical examiner and to arrange for an ambulance.
By the time Chief Schmidt returned, Ben's brother Antone Kulvinskas
had arrived. Ben told Antone that he thought the first time he was
shot was on Friday and that he had been hit in the legs and was unable
to move.

Antone spoke in Lithuanian. Ben responded in English, "Sophie Kritchman and Joe Mitchell kill [sic] me and Sophie Kritchman cut my neck." The Kulvinskas brothers continued to converse in Lithuanian. Ben reportedly said:

Sophie called me here and as soon as I came here and lie down she shot me. She asked me if I was tired and warm so I lay down. She then told me and asked me to take my coat off, and she took my coat off and she laid it on the ground and she told me to lay on it, and I did. She said I will put a handkerchief over your face so that the flies won't get in your face, or that the sun won't burn your face, and as soon as she put the handkerchief over my face she said she will go out into the road to see if anyone is coming. Then she come back in about a half a minute and she said something at that time and what the word is I don't know, and she said why do you go with me? You want to separate me from either my fellow or my man, and as soon as she said that she shot me right away. She shot me four times and threw the revolver at me.[45]

Antone asked his brother where the revolver was, and Ben motioned toward the bushes.[46] He found the revolver and gave it to Chief Schmidt.

The chief reportedly said, "My God, your brother must have attempted suicide. He shot himself and cut his throat."[47] This seems an odd assessment, but there have been many strange calls like this in the history of crime.[48]

"Why did you go with her?" Ben was asked.

He replied, "How was I to know why I was called?"

Antone asked if anyone else was there.

Ben answered, "Joe Mitchell was there. *I didn't see him* [emphasis added], Antone, but I heard him talking from behind. I knew his voice."

Ben continued, "Sophie came there half past seven or eight o'clock; I saw her pull a knife out of her stocking about that long [indicating], and she cut me in the neck/throat. I did not think I would tell it to anyone. When Sophie came there in the morning, she wanted to know whether I was alive or not and picked up a stone and threw it at me in the head.

I moved a little, and I wanted to grab this stone. Joe Mitchell drew up near me from behind and put a revolver up to my head and fired. Antone, when he shot me, then my hat flew off my head. I thought I was not alive."[49]

As to the first time he was shot, Ben elaborated, "I was shot, and I was thinking that they would probably find me dead. I made it appear that I was dead so that they wouldn't shoot me to death, and then I came conscious and I was thinking that they would find me dead in four or five days in the woods and then I picked up the paper out of my pocket and wrote out down there so it would know who it was that shot me and kilt me."[50]

This blood-smeared paper, found at the crime scene, was written in Lithuanian, and while it was difficult to decipher even with the aid of a magnifying glass, it said something to the effect that "Sophia Kritchman shot me" and "Sophie Kritchman, it seems I must die a death at your hands." The Findings of the trial judge in aid of appeal gives us this translation:

Sofe Kritchman
it seem I must die a death
your hands
at 2 after dinner, me
Kul or Kol Bransue shot
for my brother

This bloody note would prove to be a hotly contested piece of evidence at Sophie's trials.

Medical Examiner Dr. E.H. Johnson was called to the scene and ordered that Ben be transported to Saint Mary's Hospital in Waterbury.

AT THE HOSPITAL

At the hospital John F. McGrath, an assistant prosecutor for the City of Waterbury, secured a statement from the victim at around five o'clock in the afternoon, Saturday, September 18, 1909.

It appears that the statement was prepared by McGrath based on what could be elicited from Ben and that Ben signed it with an *X*.

Mitchell is only mentioned at the end of Ben's statement: "Last time [Sophie came back Saturday] with Joe Mitchell and Joe shot me once in the back of the head." There were other witnesses present when the statement was taken, and we will hear more from them later.

St. Mary's Hospital, Waterbury, Connecticut, A.C. Bosselman & Co., New York, circa 1910 (12)

STATE'S EXHIBIT 9.

I, Bronislowas Kulwinskas, being on the point
of death and without hope of recovery make the following
statement.

On Friday, Sept. 17, Sophy Crageman at whose mother's
house I boarded, asked me to take a walk in the woods.
We went out and she said to me to take off my coat and
lay on it.   I did and she said I will place a handkerchief
over your face and mouth and go and see if anyone is coming.
When she came back she said "what to hell you spoil my
company for. I am going to shoot you."   She then

(2)

shot me five times and I fell in the bushes. On Friday
night at nine o'clock she came back and found me in the
bushes and cut my throat.   Before cutting me she said
I will cut your throat and will kill myself too.   She had
a long knife.

Next day Saturday she came back and threw stone at me.
She came back 3 times. Last time with Joe Mitchell and
Joe shot me once in the back of the head.

Signed

            BRONISLOVAS   his
                     KULWINSKAS.   X mark.

Sworn to before me Sept. 18, (09.
         John F. McGrath Justice of the Peace.
Augustin A. Crane
M. J. Lawler, M.D.

Exhibit 9, Ben Kulvinskas's statement secured at the hospital by Assistant Prosecutor John F. McGrath. The findings of the trial judge refer to this as Exhibit
8, but a typewritten copy found in the file marks it as Exhibit 9. That may be
explained by the fact that there were two trials, and exhibits may have been
marked differently in each case. (13)

By the time McGrath had secured Ben's statement, the police had searched the Kritchman home and had found Sophie hiding in the cellar.[51] When she was arrested, she asked whether Joe Mitchell had been arrested.[52] She was taken to Waterbury and placed in a cell. Police searched Mitchell's room over the Mazikas & Pavolinis saloon on North Riverside Street and found a revolver. Shortly thereafter, Mitchell was spotted across the street and arrested.

From the very start, Mitchell insisted that he had not been in Union City on Friday or Saturday and knew nothing about the crime. The task for the police was to find someone who saw Mitchell in town on Friday and Saturday.

Lieutenant Thomas A. Dodds[53] (later, Captain Dodds), of the Waterbury Police Department Detective Bureau, brought Mitchell face to face with Ben Kulvinskas, and Dodds asked Ben if this was the man who had shot him.

> "Do you know this man?" Kulvinskas replied, "Ye." Then Kulvinskas was asked who it was, and he replied, "Joe Mitchell." Then Kulvinskas was asked if this Joe Mitchell was the man who shot him, and he said, "Yes." That, when he said Mitchell was the man who shot him, Mitchell threw himself back with his hands out, and he says, "Christ Almighty! I didn't do it! I don't know anything about it!" That, then, Mitchell went over to Kulvinskas and said something to him in the Lithuanian language, which the witness did not understand, whereupon the officer told Mitchell he would have to speak in English.[54]

Later Sophie was taken to Ben, and he identified her, too.[55] Ben died Saturday night.[56]

Police Work

The case did not seem to pose much of a mystery. Indeed, summaries in the *Naugatuck Daily News* published as early as September 20 and 21, 1909, listed most of the witnesses who would later appear at the trials and set out the stories that they would tell.[57]

Sophie broke down rather quickly during Deputy Coroner William Makepeace's investigation. Although the circumstances pointed to Sophie as the instigator of the crime and an active participant, she attempted to shift blame onto Mitchell—but the evidence suggested that the two had acted in concert and in accordance with a plan.[58] Sophie's story was that she had agreed to lure Ben to the scene of the crime on Friday morning, where Mitchell would be waiting in the bushes. In her initial version, the plan was to stun and rob Ben[59] and then she and Mitchell would make away together. According to Sophie, Mitchell did all the shooting[60]—although it was rumored that she had initially admitted that she shot once but had been compelled to do so by Mitchell.[61]

Sophie's story was hardly seamless. Neither she nor Mitchell had taken a big roll of money that Ben had had in his pockets.[62] She had also given an inconsistent version—that Mitchell had come upon her and Ben "unaware" and that Mitchell had threatened to kill her if she exposed him.[63]

Lawyers and judges know that statements to authorities made by partners in crime while they are in custody are notoriously unreliable, even if some of the statements are self-inculpatory. Falsehood will be mixed with truth to shift blame to the absent confederate.[64] As all this with Sophie and Mitchell was unfolding in the local papers, a story from Georgia was reported in one of the same papers at the same time: *Girl Lied—Story Sent Sweetheart to Jail for Twenty Years.*[65]

During a search of Sophie's personal effects, a number of love letters were found. They were mostly from Mitchell, but some were from a Dr. A.K. Rutzkauskas of Chicago.[66] Sophie seemed to have an excess of beaus, but it turned out that she was not alone in having multiple love interests. It was known that Ben had a relationship with a Mary Pokos (also spelled Poekas or Puekas) and that the two were planning marriage. It was also reported that Ben had told Sophie of his marriage plans on the morning of the murder.[67] Some were of the opinion that Sophie suffered from delusions about her relationships with all these men and that it might be evidence of mental instability.[68] Many speculated that Sophie had been motivated by jealousy.[69]

Dr. Rutzkauskas was something of a puzzle. He began his correspondence with Sophie after reading newspaper accounts of her plight. He seems to have been one of those characters who surfaces in high-profile cases, like today's groupies who flock to convicts on death row. When the letters back and forth shifted to a foreign language (Polish, the papers said), the authorities began to hold up Sophie's mail so that it could be examined by an interpreter.[70]

As the investigation continued, the story got more complicated. Witnesses came forward who said that they saw some people going to the crime scene on Friday and that they were followed by Kulvinskas, but it was proving difficult to establish that Mitchell was one of them or that he was there on Friday. The police did have the statement of Sophie's twelve-year-old sister, Mamie, that Mitchell was at the Kritchman home on Friday afternoon. The police thought that they also had evidence that Sophie and Mitchell had come to Union City on the same streetcar on Saturday. A witness, Mrs. Mary Murphy, said that she had seen Sophie and a man she thought was Mitchell walking in the direction of the crime scene on Saturday morning.[71] On the other hand, Lithuanians supportive of Mitchell claimed that he was not in Union City on Friday. And a Joseph Raytkiewich of Naugatuck, a friend of Ben, claimed that he had talked with Ben when he was being taken away from the crime scene and that Ben had told him that Sophie had shot him and cut his throat but that Mitchell had had nothing to do with it.[72]

The star witness for the prosecution would be ten-year-old Victoria

Dalton, one of Sophie's music students.[73] According to Victoria, Sophie came to Victoria's house on Friday afternoon around one o'clock and asked to take her for a walk. Victoria's mother agreed so long as they did not go "past McDermott's," sometimes referred to as "McDermott's farm," which was probably located at 61 Spring Street where Andrew F. McDermott had a grocery and meat market, along with a garden. However, Sophie took the girl beyond that all the way to the crime scene, where she said, "Wait here." Victoria said that Sophie took a stick and poked something in the bushes, whereupon a man called out, "Anthony! Anthony!" (the name of Ben's brother). Sophie said, "This is Sophie," but the man kept crying for Anthony.[74]

Victoria told authorities:

> Sophie then came out [of the bushes] when I began to cry, and she said "It's only some old tramp. Wait until I get a stone." But I began to cry so much that she finally went back with me towards home. And she told me never to say anything about that tramp or we would both be arrested and sent to jail. She told me later that if I told my mother she would kill me. On the way back, she said "Let's sit down." We did and then she pulled out a *knife or razor* [emphasis added] or something from her stocking. It looked more like a razor.[75]

One speculates that Sophie was using the walk with the child as a cover to see whether Ben was still alive, but her actions, including her threats, seem quite irrational.

Needless to say, the child could not keep the secret. On Friday night, Victoria seemed anxious and had no appetite. On Saturday, Victoria and her mother were standing at a window when the ambulance transporting Ben drove past the house. Victoria burst into tears and told her mother, "Oh, Sophie and I know something about that."

As things developed, the McDermotts and their daughter came forward to report that they had seen Sophie returning from the direction of the crime scene earlier that morning, walking hurriedly as she looked back toward the scene from time to time.

Further investigation turned up a report that sometime later Sophie had gone to Waterbury and purchased a .32 caliber revolver at S.M. "Samuel" Schneer's store at 198 South Main Street in Waterbury.[76] This revolver was found early in the investigation, and all the cartridges had been fired. The authorities were told that before she paid for it, she asked the store clerk if the weapon would kill a man, and she supposedly said, "All right. I have a man to kill." If she actually said this, it was a startling admission.

Sophie would claim that she met up with Mitchell and that the two sneaked back to the Shady Nook where Mitchell then shot Ben in the head. Based on the statement of little Victoria, the police believed that Sophie had cut Ben's throat with a razor.[77]

Sophie's mother contributed to the case against Mitchell by suggesting a possible motive for the crime. She reported that Ben had told her that he thought Mitchell would kill him if he spent too much time with Sophie. Ben's brother Antone also provided an apparent link in the chain by reporting that someone had gotten into the trunk in his room at the Kritchman place and had stolen his pistol. Antone suspected Mitchell, who he thought had been in his room the Wednesday before the killing.[78]

On September 23, 1909, Sophia Kritchman and Joe Mitchell (as Joseph Peczinitis) were jointly indicted for the first-degree murder of Bronick (or Bronislaw or Bronislow) "Ben" Kulvinskas. (The names were spelled several ways throughout the history of the case.[79])

Defense lawyers in multiple defendant cases will ordinarily file motions to sever their clients' cases for separate trial. This is particularly important if the moving defendant appears less culpable—or at least claims to be less culpable—than the other. Sophie's lawyers were successful in getting her a separate trial, and Sophie's trial would go first. This would be an advantage to her. Sophie was a female with whom jurors of the time might have sympathized. Moreover, she could cast blame on Mitchell, the absent defendant, who would not be in a position to answer unless he turned state's evidence.

At some point during her stay in jail while awaiting trial, Sophie asked to have a piano moved into her cell. Instead, she was given a "canned variety" of music. A "hurdy-gurdy was stationed near the police station,

Newspaper article, "Is This Pretty Girl a Human or a Demon?," with photograph of Sophia [Sophie] Kritchman, *The Star* (Seattle, Washington), October 6, 1910 (14)

and the crank was turned by the various news gatherers."[80] Whether this was done to mock her is not clear.

From the start, reporters noted Sophie's peculiar behavior. Some characterized her as calm and unconcerned, laughing and joking as she was transported in custody.[81] While in jail, she complained only of the absence of a piano.[82] In marked contrast to these assessments, it was rumored that a weeping Sophie had been seen early the Friday morning of the crime in the cemetery where her half sister was buried.[83] Locals talked of the death of Mrs. William Batinski, the half sister, six years earlier. The woman was said to have been "unbalanced," and one day she was found "writhing in agony as a result of taking a large quantity of Paris green (in those days used as a rodenticide or insecticide)." Mrs. Batinski died before any aid could reach her.[84]

Physicians who took note of Sophie's indifference speculated that her defense would be insanity.[85] How else could her role in the crime be explained? Newspapers as far away as Seattle, Washington, would soon pick up the story with lurid headlines—*Is This Pretty Girl a Human or a Demon?*[86]

Waterbury awaited a sensational trial, and some folks were cashing in. "Souvenir post cards bearing a likeness of Sophia Kritchman…[were]… printed. The picture post card men evidently believe[ed] in being right up to date."[87]

PART TWO

The First Trial Begins

The Curtain Rises

As her trial neared, Sophie gave every indication that she expected to be acquitted. Perhaps her confidence was buoyed by the fact that this was reportedly "the first time in the criminal history of Connecticut that a woman as young and beautiful as…[Sophie had]…been obliged to plead to a capital offense."[88] Furthermore, as far as anyone knew, Connecticut had never executed a woman.[89] Actually that was not the fact.[90]

Sophie busied herself with the selection of her "costumes" (a word used by the reporters) with the advice of lawyer William Kennedy, a former state senator.

William Kennedy, Connecticut lawyer and former member
of the Connecticut State Senate (1889–1901). In 1913, Kennedy
was elected U.S. Representative from Connecticut. (15)

When she was called before the coroner, she had dressed all in black and had given the appearance of a woman of more mature years.[91] Now she had a stage director—her advocate.

Kennedy told the press that she would not be "dre[ssed] as tho[ugh] she were to attend a society function in Brooklyn." Sophie would make her first appearance in a blue gown that came to her shoe tops, and she would wear a hat with a "jaunty plume or two." By today's standards it all seems a bit spectacular, but at the time the reporters described her as looking like a "simple school girl…just a year or two out of school…. She smil[ed] in a bored, impersonal way as though attendance upon the proceedings were an irksome necessity, but quite devoid of really unpleasant possibilities."[92]

Sophie even spoke of plans for the stage, alluding to offers from vaudeville.[93] Perhaps she had followed the sensational trials of New York City showgirl Nan Patterson, who had been acquitted of the murder of gambler and man-about-town Caesar Young in 1905. Nan's trials had been fashion shows and Nan had boasted of her career opportunities in the theater, but there was a big difference between the cases. Nan had had a plausible (barely so, but surprisingly successful) claim of self-defense.[94] What would Sophie and Kennedy come up with?

Right up to the start of the trial there was talk that Sophie's defense team would drop the argument that she and Ben had been ambushed by Mitchell and that resort would be had to a plea of insanity.[95] That was not to be. The plea would be not guilty. Supposedly, this is what Sophie told lawyer Kennedy:

I did not kill Ben, Mr. Kennedy. I am innocent, and you must make those men believe me. I loved Ben and I would have married him if Joe Mitchell had not come between us. Oh, why do they keep me here when I told them I did not kill Ben. I told them the truth when they questioned me in the police station, but I never said I had killed Ben. Oh, Mr. Kennedy, make them believe me and let me go home to my dear mother. I will be so good and I will work hard to pay back all the expense she has been forced into because I did not think.[96]

So she *loved Ben*. Authorities had cause to be skeptical. They would be told by one of her friends that she had said she was going to marry Joe Mitchell.[97]

Lawyer Kennedy told the reporters:

I believe Sophia is the victim of circumstance. I have had many conferences with her and every time she has protested her innocence. I told her I must have the entire truth if I was to attempt her defense, and she has promised me solemn vows that she is innocent of the murder of Kulvinskas. We will go on trial on her plea that she is innocent and had no part in any plot to murder Kulvinskas.[98]

As jury selection opened on January 25, Sophie was interviewed by a reporter from the *Waterbury Republican*. Again, her comments were quite remarkable. The reporter described Sophie being "as naïve and frank as a school girl" but at times smiling "like an Oriental coquet [sic]." She told reporters that as her counsel asked questions of the potential jurors, she could not help but laugh at some of the replies:

Some of the men seemed to think that I could do such a terrible thing. I suppose I will have lots of things to consider from now on, but I have such faith in Mr. Kennedy…I have not lived like other girls who have been brought into court cases. All my time was spent around a convent. You see I graduated from ninth grade in the public school and I have such a love for music that I was a good pupil. How I wish I could see the dear sisters of the Convent of St. Peter's church in Hartford. You know where it is, just opposite the South Green. If I were only back there now how happy I would be…

When asked about her love letters from the doctor in Chicago, she continued:

Letters? Well, I should say I did. I received hundreds of them, and he makes love so grand in his letters. No, I have never seen him, but he says some of his people know me and I love to get letters. In love with him? No, you can't call it that. I don't want any more lovers until I get out of here.[99]

Sophie *was* an actress of sorts, but how good an actress remained to be seen.

The *voir dire* (jury selection) went pretty much as one would have expected. Prosecutor John P. Kellogg's strategy was to get jurors with prior experience, particularly in criminal trials in which guilty verdicts had been returned.

Kennedy was meticulous in his questioning, and he wanted no one on the jury who had "formed an opinion." One juror indicated that he thought the fact that Sophie had been indicted was evidence of guilt, and he was quickly rejected. Eswain Smith, who appeared anxious to serve on the jury, was examined for some time and was successfully challenged by the defense. Edgar Beadle, a public office holder who had previously served on a capital case, was likewise given the boot by Kennedy. Andrew Culver, a farmer from Beacon Falls, was called and said he was not familiar with the case, but after he reported that he was married and was the father of three girls, he was just as quickly rejected by the prosecution. Ultimately all the talesmen who came from Naugatuck and Waterbury

Dr. A.K. Rutzkauskas, Chicago, Illinois (16))

Prosecutor John P. Kellogg (17)

were excused after a bench conference.[100] As jury selection continued, it was clear that Judge Howard J. Curtis would excuse any juror who was opposed to the death penalty or who would have scruples against the infliction of the death sentence upon a young woman.[101]

During the examination of one juror, the reporters—and presumably others—took note.

> [Sophie] wanted to make a suggestion to Attorney [John H.] Cassidy [her junior defense counsel] and turning quickly she put up both hands and encircled the neck of the youthful counsel. Pulling his head down to her lips she acted as if she were about to impart a kiss. Mr. Cassidy is noted for his bashfulness among the fair sex and he tried to pull away, but Sophie had a strangle hold. "I like that man, Mr. Cassidy," whispered Sophia, indicating a juror who had just been accepted by Attorney Kennedy and then she relaxed her hold, while Mr. Cassidy cautioned her not to "do that again," at the same time casting a glance around the room to see if the action had been noted. His inspection satisfied him that the move was observed and for the next five minutes he devoted his attention to making notes.[102]

Judge Howard J. Curtis (18)

Attorney John H. Cassidy, junior defense counsel for
Sophia [Sophie] Kritchman (19)

Sophie in the Dock

Sophie's trial was the best show in town, but it was not the only show. This headline was on the front page of the *Waterbury Republican*, above the fold, alongside the Kritchman coverage.

BRUTE'S TWO WIVES MEET IN HOSPITAL
Bride Who Was Cast Into
Well Embraces Another
Spouse of John Marok
POLICE LEARN THAT HE MARRIED THRICE[103]

The denizens of Connecticut were being treated to several good helpings of terror these days. Fortunately, a Post Toasties ad on the next page provided some soothing counterpoint.

Get the Happy Mood.
Post Toasties
With cream or fruit
For a breakfast starter, are sure
to produce it.
And there's a lot in starting
the day right.
You're bound to hand happi-
ness to someone as you go along—
the more sunshine you give, the more you get.
Post Toasties will increase the
happiness of the whole family.

John Marok, like the cynic, might have answered that happiness, like the truth, lies at the bottom of a well.

Shortly after the noon recess the trial proper began with the reading of the indictment—a long and tedious business. Sophie appeared to listen carefully to each word. When the clerk finished with his recitation, she turned to the jury and smiled. Prosecutor Kellogg then gave his opening statement. According to the convention at the time, the defense reserved its opening statement.

The first witness called was George C. Ham, a civil engineer and surveyor from Naugatuck, who provided a detailed map of the area where Ben had been found. Defense lawyer Kennedy engaged in a meticulous and lengthy cross-examination. The engineer's testimony was followed by that of Police Chief Schmidt, who described the scene of the crime and the condition of the victim and who recounted his own activities as he waited for the ambulance that would take Ben to Saint Mary's hospital.

Prosecutor Kellogg approached the witness, Police Chief Schmidt: "Showing you a piece of paper. Did you ever see that before?" It was the bloodstained piece of paper that bore Ben's accusation that Sophie had shot him. The witness identified the document as the one found at the scene, although he could not say who had found it first. Testimony was then elicited to the effect that the bushes were so thick where the body was found that they could only have been parted with difficulty. This was verified by a photo. Sophie had told police that Mitchell had forced his way through the bushes to the point where Ben was lying, and this evidence was presumably intended to undermine her story.

The next witness was Dr. Dudley B. Deming, a microscopist who had performed certain tests on the bloodstained paper to decipher the writing on it. Dr. Deming was cross-examined aggressively by Kennedy, who objected to the way the doctor had arrived at his conclusions, paying particular attention to how the doctor had read a portion of one of the sentences.

The prosecution then called Dr. A.A. Crane, who had come to the hospital to attend to Ben. He used a large, colored, life-size chart of a man to illustrate each of the wounds. This chart can be seen on illustration 20.

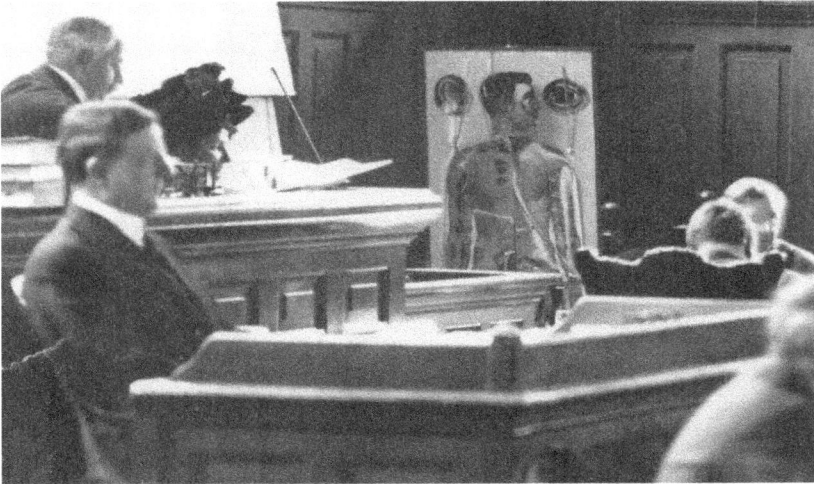

Life-size chart of man used during the trial to illustrate each of the wounds to the victim, Ben Kulvinskas, detail from Courtroom Scene: Trial of Sophia Kritchman and Joe Mitchell, 1910. Unknown photographer. (20)

As Dr. Crane testified, Sophie "leaned forward in the chair...her breast heaved and her breath came in short gasps. Her hands opened and clutched convulsively at the arms of the chair in which she was seated."[104] A female spectator fled the courtroom, explaining when questioned that "I would soon lose my appetite for supper if I should remain here."[105] Yet there was a moment of comic relief when Dr. Crane remarked as he looked at his chart that showed the anatomy of a man, with stickers identifying the bullet wounds, "One of the wounds has dropped off."

The prosecution then laid the foundation for the introduction of Ben's dying declarations. Dr. Crane testified that after he ascertained that Ben had only a few hours to live, he notified police officials and the mayor of this fact. He described the victim's condition:

The patient was very faint and he had evidently been bleeding freely. He had a gash in his throat about five inches in length. There were other wounds in the body and the clothing was matted with dried blood. His pulse was very poor. His extremities [were] getting cold and he was evidently mortally wounded, so I notified the mayor that he was in a dying condition. I remained with the patient until 6 o'clock and then left him in the charge of Dr. Pomeroy. When I returned at 9 o'clock the man was dead.[106]

When Dr. Crane described the wound to the throat and illustrated the way it might have been inflicted, "many in the courtroom shuddered." However, he went on to testify that Ben could have recovered from the wound and that only two of the twelve bullet wounds would have caused death. In his opinion:

[T]he cause of death was shock and hemorrhage caused by one bullet passing thru the lung and liver, causing the right lung to collapse. The wound in the skull was the lesser, but the bullet entered at the back of the skull, fracturing and splintering the bone and penetrating the brain. Either wound would have caused death.[107]

Kennedy tried to shift the blame from his client, Sophie.

"It would have required a strong hand to make such a wound, wouldn't it?" Kennedy asked.

Dr. Crane did not think so.

"It couldn't be made by a child, could it?" asked Kennedy.

"Yes, I think it could," replied Dr. Crane.

"But don't you know a man must have done it?" Kennedy demanded.

"No sir, I do not," Dr. Crane replied.[108]

The physician's testimony was quite effective and left no openings for the defense. However, toward the end of his cross-examination, Kennedy suddenly stopped and asked:

"By the way, how tall was Kulvinskas, doctor?"

Dr. Crane responded, "Six feet."

Kennedy continued his cross-examination, "Then the person who could inflict a wound at the base of the skull of a man six feet tall must have been nearly of equal height?"

"Yes sir," answered Dr. Crane.

"Sophia, stand up." Kennedy instructed. "Doctor, would it be possible for a frail child like that to have inflicted such a wound on a man six feet tall?" Kennedy asked Dr. Crane.

"N-no," Dr. Crane answered.

Kennedy concluded, "That's all. You may sit down Sophia."[109]

The overconfident physician had been had. Later the evidence would show that Ben was almost certainly not standing when the death wounds were inflicted; but for the moment it seemed that the defense had scored.

THE BLOODY NOTE

Lawyer Kennedy's minor victory was short-lived. When Dr. Crane was recalled to the stand, he wished to correct some of his earlier testimony regarding his visits to the hospital after having his "memory refreshed" and he also wanted to change his testimony that a tall man must have inflicted the head wound. He opined that the wound could have been inflicted by a smaller person if the victim had been sitting or lying on the ground. Although the cross-examination was *sharp*, the earlier damage had been repaired.[110] Now the case would take another turn and provide another short-lived victory for the defense.

The issue before the court was whether the bloodstained note should be admitted as Ben's dying declaration that pointed to Sophie as the principal assailant. Antone Kulvinskas authenticated the note as being the one he had found at the scene of the crime, and he identified the handwriting as his brother Ben's. The murder trial would now turn into a battle of the experts that would first be fought outside of the jury's presence.[111]

Before the jurors would be permitted to see the bloody note, the judge would take testimony to see whether a sufficient foundation had been laid to support its admissibility. If he allowed the note to be admitted, the same evidence and argument that had been made to him could then be presented to the jury, and the jurors would determine the weight to be given the evidence of the bloody note. That is to say, the jurors might downplay the importance of the note if they thought it was unreliable evidence—if they accepted the argument that it had been written by a victim who was not in his senses at the time or that it had been written by someone else.

During the hearing before Judge Curtis, Dr. John Hackett, a defense microscopist, challenged Dr. Deming's opinion and denied that it was possible to use the microscope to correctly make out the letters on the note. On the other hand, M.R. Malinowsky, "a widely known interpreter of the Lithuanian tongue," provided his translation of the words on the note, getting a full sense of the words after consulting with Dr. Deming. According to Malinowsky, the words appeared to say:

> Sophie Kriezman, it seems must die death your hands. At two after dinner. Me kol. Branzue shot for my brother. I your Ro-Sofe me shot.

Malinowsky translated this cryptic message as saying:

> Sophie Kriezman, it seems I must die a death at your hands. At two after dinner me Kul. Branzue was shot. For my brother I your Ro__, Sofe shot me.

A reporter for the *Hartford Courant* was not impressed and described Malinowsky as "smart," in the pejorative sense of the word. "There was 'smartness' in his patronizing attitude [o]n the stand, his glib replies, his eagerness in combat with Attorney Kennedy. Testifying was his profession, and he was an expert [at that]."[112]

Kennedy subjected the self-assured expert witness Malinowsky to a blistering cross-examination. As an experienced cross-examiner, Kennedy used leading questions in an effort to elicit *yes or no* answers. The expert became defensive, and he began to "retort sharply" to Kennedy.[113] This was a mistake, because Judge Curtis rebuked Malinowsky and told him to answer the questions without evasion.[114]

Next Kennedy followed up, first by calling Joseph A. Shunskis, a Union City barber and court interpreter, who was not only skilled in the translation of Lithuanian but also very knowledgeable of courtroom procedure. He went so far as to say that "it was impossible to define the language in the note."[115]

Then, presumably as a surprise to all, Kennedy called Sophie to the stand. She testified that she was well versed in Lithuanian, the language of her parents, and had been tutored in Lithuanian by Ben. She "presented the appearance of a trim looking high school girl about to rehearse a part in a play. There was not a trace of fear on her face. On the contrary, she seemed to be more self possest [sic] than any woman in the room."[116] Her testimony was reported word for word by a *Waterbury Republican* reporter, who noted her demeanor, indicated in brackets below:

"Sophia, where did you live before you got into this trouble?" Kennedy asked.

"At home with my mother, on Anderson Street in Union City." Sophie answered. [a tremor in the voice]

Kennedy continued, "Is that in the boro [sic] of Naugatuck?"

Sophie replied, "Yes sir." [a tremble of the voice]

"Did you know Ben Kulvinskas?" Kennedy asked.

Sophie answered, "I did. He boarded with my mother about four years ago. There was some trouble, and my mother put him out. He returned to the house about ten months ago an—"

"Never mind that now. Did you know then Ben Kulvinskas?" Kennedy inquired.

Sophie responded, "I did." [appearing to be on the verge of breaking down]

Kennedy continued, "Did Ben Kulvinskas board at your house, Sophia?"

Sophie answered, "Y-yes, h-he d-did."

"You were in his company some?" Kennedy asked.

Sophie replied, "Y-yes, I-I-I was." [half sob, light flow of tears]

"You were familiar with his handwriting?" Kennedy asked.

Sophie answered, "Oh, yes, he taught me to write in the Lithuanian language." [beginning to recover]

Kennedy continued, "Calling your attention to Exhibit 2 of the state, I will ask you if any part of the writing is in the hand of the deceased?"

Sophie replied, "Not a word." [a moment before tearful but now speaking "as clear as a bell"]

"One more thing, Sophia. Was Kulvinskas a poor speller?" Kennedy inquired.

"No. On the contrary, he was very correct in his spelling." Sophia answered.

Kennedy asked, "What is the proper way to spell the word 'me' in the Lithuanian language?"

Sophie replied, "M-a-n-e."

Kennedy to Kellogg: "You may inquire." [a smile of victory on Kennedy's face][117]

It is reported that Kellogg started to rise but then declined to cross-examine at this point. Sophie, with "a look of triumph upon her face," returned to her seat and whispered to young lawyer Cassidy, "Did I do alright, Mr. Cassidy?" "Fine, fine," he reassured her."[118]

Then came Judge Curtis's ruling:

I will not allow the paper to go to the jury either as a dying declaration or as part of the *res gestae*, but I will receive it in evidence
to the court to be used in connection with other evidence upon
which you, Mr. Kellogg, may intend to introduce to show the
physical condition of the man at the time other declarations were
made later, which I presume will be claimed as dying declarations.[119]

The defense and the press thought this ruling was an important win
for Kennedy.[120] For the first time in the case, Prosecutor Kellogg *excepted*
(noted his disagreement for the record) from one of the judge's rulings.[121]
Still, the note would later prove to have some value.

After this ruling, in the afternoon session, Antone continued his
testimony about the events at the crime scene and his finding of the
revolver there, which he identified as the weapon that was missing from
his trunk. As Antone continued, Sophie went into a "fit of weeping"
and was on the verge of hysteria.[122] This was quite a mood swing. The
examination ended for the day.

As the day's business was going on, visitors to the proceedings seemed
to show a particular interest in what little Victoria Dalton would have to
say when called to the stand. A reporter noted, "[S]he romps and plays
about the court house during recess and child-like, does not realize what
an important part her testimony is to play in the trial."[123]

DYING DECLARATIONS

In addition to the bloody note, there were multiple other supposed dying declarations made by Ben. Other statements included those made at the crime scene to Walter H. Roberts when Ben was first found and those made in the presence of Antone and three other fellow countrymen. There were also statements made at the hospital, including the written one taken by Assistant Prosecutor John F. McGrath, as well as a statement in question-and-answer (Q&A) form taken at the hospital and transcribed by court reporter Thomas W. Walsh (later known as the Walsh Transcript).

The first statement to be offered by the prosecution was the rather lengthy story told to Antone and three of Ben's friends when they arrived

Attorney James M. Lynch (21)

at the crime scene. "The smile faded from the face of Sophia Kritchman" when the testimony of Joseph Raytkiewich, a Naugatuck saloon keeper, was reported to include these words spoken by Ben:

> First we walked from the house; we come as far here. I took off my coat and lay down on the ground. Sophia said 'I guess I will lie along side of you.' Then she take a handkerchief and say 'I will put this over your face so the flies will not bite you.' Then I was shot.[124]

However, only one of the three friends provided this damning evidence. The other two testified that they had not heard the conversation. By way of cross-examination, Kennedy accused Raytkiewich of being in league with "all the rum sellers and bartenders to place the crime at the door of this little girl for the purpose of aiding Joe Mitchell." Kennedy railed against the witnesses, accusing them of "com[ing] very close to the border line of perjury." Sophie insisted that one of the friends who claimed to understand no English could in fact speak it. Later in the trial Kennedy would repeat his charges that rum runners and members of the Lithuanian community were engaged in some kind of conspiracy in support of Mitchell. Mitchell was a member of an organization of "so-called Independent Catholics," which was raising funds for his defense. Attorney James M. Lynch was retained as Mitchell's defense counsel, and a rumor circulated that Mitchell might turn state's evidence.[125]

Overall, Raytkiewich held up pretty well under Kennedy's cross-examination. He faltered a bit when Kennedy attempted to impeach him by suggesting that only last Tuesday, he had told Mrs. Kritchman that he couldn't remember a word Ben Kulvinskas had said. Unable to get Raytkiewich to concede that the conversation took place, Kennedy returned to the witness's dealings in the rum business. Then Kennedy demanded that Raytkiewich repeat the story that he had told the jury. The witness "leaned far back in his chair" and repeated his testimony, as Kennedy had insisted. Again, Kennedy would blunder.

"Did the deceased say anything else?" Kennedy asked Raytkiewich.

"Yes," Raytkiewich answered. "He said, 'Sophia Kritchman shot me. Sophia Kritchman cut my throat.'"

Kennedy then asked, "To whom did you tell this story before you told it here to the jury?"

Raytkiewich replied, "I told it to you, Mr. Kennedy, when you got on the trolley car near Platts Mills [a business and a road] last September."[126]

Enraged, Kennedy tried to pin Raytkiewich down as to this alleged conversation, when it took place, and what its exact content was. Prosecutor Kellogg came to Raytkiewich's aid with the objection that the cross-examiner was harrying the witness, and the court sustained the objection. As a matter of ethics, trial counsel should not allow himself to become a witness, so Kennedy was at something of a disadvantage. Raytkiewich managed to inject that he had made the same statements to John M. Sweeney, a prosecutor, and to Police Chief John R. Schmidt, both of Naugatuck.

Kennedy might have moved to strike this volunteered testimony as nonresponsive and improperly self-bolstering, but instead he shifted gears. As he continued the cross-examination, Kennedy moved closer to the witness to intimidate him.

"What did you say to Mrs. Kritchman, this old mother, the mother of this little girl in this court room last Tuesday?" Kennedy asked.

Raytkiewich answered, "I-I don't remember."

To which Kennedy responded, "You remember everything that transpired in the woods in Union City last September, but you don't remember what occurred in this room last Tuesday. Do you want to make that statement to this jury?"

"I don't remember what I said. I might have said something," Raytkiewich replied.

Kennedy continued, moving closer to the witness, "Did you tell this old woman to have her daughter say she shot Kulvinskas and that would make it easier for Joe Mitchell and her daughter could be sent to an asylum?"

"I never mentioned Joe Mitchell. I might have mentioned to have Sophie sent to an asylum," Raytkiewich testified. [*shifting in his chair*]

Kennedy moved closer to the witness and continued his cross-examination, "That's all...but wait a minute. Showing you a photograph, did you ever see that face [of Joe Mitchell] before?"

Raytkiewich replied, "No."

"Did you ever see Joe Mitchell?" asked Kennedy.

"No," Raytkiewich answered.

"Did you ever see the person who is accused of being implicated with this girl in this crime?" Kennedy asked, moving still closer. Raytkiewich responded, "No."[127]

The witness was trying to stick to his story, but it would be hard for the jury to believe that he was not acquainted with Mitchell.

Did Kennedy have a good faith basis for asking the questions about a conversation with Mrs. Kritchman, or was he just throwing a skunk into the jury box? It is unethical to ask a question without a good faith basis. One cannot rely on innuendo, and one would ordinarily have expected a cross-examiner like Kennedy to follow up this attempted impeachment with his own witness—Sophie's mother, Mrs. Kritchman, for example. The nature of the attacks suggests that calling Mrs. Kritchman to prove that Raytkiewich was lying about his possible bias or interest in the outcome of the case would have been permissible, as the matter seems important enough—not collateral. She was not called.

Back on direct examination, Prosecutor Kellogg turned his attention to the statements Ben had made at the hospital, including the Q&A taken down by stenographer Walsh. Kellogg took testimony from Dr. Crane, Walsh, Deputy Coroner Makepeace, and Dr. Pomeroy. Kellogg did his best to establish that Ben was of sufficiently sound mind to understand that he was dying and to understand and respond to the questions put to him; however, it is fair to say that the evidence was conflicting. Dr. Crane said that Ben seemed bright and capable of answering questions, but at times Ben rambled. Later in his testimony Dr. Crane said that "about a third of the time…[Ben] did not know what he was saying." Still later in his testimony the doctor said that the victim was rational about seven-eighths of the time. Deputy Coroner Makepeace claimed that the victim appeared to be rational "during the greater part of the examination" and that Ben said he was going to die. However, by means of cross-examination by omission, Kennedy pointed out that the witness's contemporaneous notes contained no such statement.[128] Kennedy then called Police Chief Schmidt and asked whether Ben had told Chief Schmidt that he believed that his death was near. Chief Schmidt replied in the negative.[129]

Kennedy's arguments throughout were that Ben never manifested any sign that he knew he was going to die, that his brother Antone would have heard him say something to that effect if Ben had said it, since he had been at Ben's side the whole time (Kennedy had gotten Antone to agree that the victim had not told him anything about dying), and that Ben had not been of sufficient mind to apprehend or appreciate the questions put to him. Kennedy was arguing that the evidentiary foundation for the admission of a dying declaration had not been laid.

Despite his efforts, the judge admitted the written statement of Ben that had been signed with an *X*.[130] Sophie apparently understood that this was a blow to the defense. "Her tiny fist clenched tightly and she was heard to whisper into the ear of her junior counsel, 'Well, the jury must get it after all, I suppose?'"[131] Sophie regained some of her cheerfulness and apparently told reporters, "Wait until I get an opportunity to tell my story and I will be able to prove my innocence. I don't want the public to judge me too harshly. My counsel is putting up a grand fight and I place my trust and confidence in them."[132]

Still, other damning evidence presented by the prosecution included the testimony of Elmer French that Sophie had tried unsuccessfully to borrow money from him, presumably to buy a gun. Sophie locked her eyes on him and sneered.[133] Mrs. Kate Sodolosky of Union City testified that Sophie called on her Saturday morning and borrowed five dollars, explaining that she had lost her money at church and needed car fare.[134] The clerk at S.M. Schneer's pawnshop at 198 South Main, Waterbury, whose name was Louis Schneer (he was apparently a relative of the shop's owner), testified that Sophie had purchased a pistol from him and that he showed her how to use it.[135] He also testified that Sophie asked for one that would kill.[136]

Kennedy was allowed to interrupt this testimony and to have the witness demonstrate the operation of the pistol with a similar gun. The clerk pulled back the hammer before pulling the trigger, but Kennedy countered by intimating that shots could only be fired rapidly by repeatedly pulling the trigger and that Sophie was not strong enough to pull the trigger.[137] Firing the weapon in a double-action mode *would* require a longer and heavier trigger pull.

Prosecutor Kellogg pressed on with the testimony of Victoria Dalton, who gave an account of her walk with Sophie to a place near the Shady Nook. She also told of hearing the voice calling for Antone. One account states that when Victoria, in the course of her testimony, said that Sophie was a favorite of all the little girls of Union City, Sophie broke down and wept.[138] Without a transcript of this trial, Victoria's exact testimony regarding what Sophie had pulled from her stocking cannot be ascertained. From newspaper copy relating to the second trial, it appears that Victoria did not clearly mention a razor or a knife but instead referred to a garter or ribbon.

Kennedy scored another point when he was able to get Judge Curtis to exclude much of the testimony of Walter H. Roberts, who had been brought to the crime scene by the boys who came upon Ben on Saturday. Roberts testified that Ben told Roberts that he knew he was dying, but Roberts became totally confused when Kennedy confronted him with the coroner's report in which he had failed to mention this or many other facts he now put before the jury.[139]

Mrs. McDermott and Canfield Booth, a local man, both testified that they saw Sophie pass their homes in the direction of the crime scene. Their testimony was supported by wood dealer Anson Sanford who said he saw Sophie walking to the woods on Friday, with Ben following after her. He also said that he was at the scene with Antone and Ben's friends the next day and that he had identified the gun found at the scene. Sanford's son, Samuel, testified that he heard shots late Friday afternoon, about five o'clock. He said that the shots "sounded to me, coming as rapid as any fellow could fire a revolver." A Mr. John Brennen heard four or five shots on Friday afternoon, and Henry C. Roberts, a milk vendor, heard some shots rapidly fired around eleven o'clock on Saturday morning.[140]

Kennedy had some fun with Mrs. McDermott, who under "merciless questioning" was forced to make at least six contradictions in her own testimony. She had also contradicted young Sanford by placing the gunshots between two and three o'clock. She shifted in the witness chair and resorted to the layman's refuge of "I don't remember."[141] Sophie reportedly played an active role in the cross-examination by giving suggestions to her counsel.

Mr. McDermott testified ineffectually, while constantly chewing a plug of tobacco. There were outbreaks of laughter while he was on the stand.

At the end of the day, Sophie was laughing and smiling. A reporter quoted her as saying that she was so confident that she would go free that she had already planned a trip to Florida.[142] The *Hartford Courant* reported her saying:

> It was one of the happiest days I have spent since I was arrested. I could not help laughing at some of the testimony and I feel as though I was going to be discharged. Ever since childhood I have always had a premonition of what was coming: when it was for the best I had a pain about my heart and tonight that pain is there, but I am so happy. I had to laugh at Mrs. McDermott. She has known me since childhood and she was always so funny.[143]

She hugged her mother and little sister, and she tried to hug lawyer Cassidy, but he shied away. She said that she was glad that Roberts's testimony was "shut out" because "he always was against her."[144]

Kennedy did win the argument on a point of evidence. Sophie had been dragged to the hospital involuntarily, and Kennedy was able to persuade the judge that it would not be proper to admit into evidence anything she had said or done at the bedside when confronted by Ben's accusations. In other words, the things she said or did could not be admitted as *adoptive admissions*—that she had accepted the truth of the accusation by not speaking up and rejecting it. As the judge put it:

> I don't think she would be expected to make any response as to what was said to her while she was under arrest and while she was standing there with the two officers.[145]

By this time the *Kritchman* case was getting national attention. Newspapers as far away as California followed the progress of the case, fascinated by the dying declarations.[146] Back home, crowd control was getting to be a problem. "Fake reporters" had to be removed from the courtroom and put out with the "sidewalk brigade."[147] The courtroom was packed with women who brought their lunches and craned to get a look at Sophie and comment on her appearance. Many women from out of town trundled in from their shopping with large packages, which presented something of a logistical problem for court officers.[148] Reporters noted, "[O]ne out of every ten of the women are sharp featured and without a grain of sympathy."[149]

The Defense Opens

As the defense opened its case, it was clear that there was not going to be any claim of insanity. Instead, blame for the killing would be shifted to Joe Mitchell. At least three witnesses would testify that they saw Mitchell with Sophie on the road leading to the place where Ben was found. That is not to say that the defense would not try to play on Sophie's mental state. The suggestion would be that Mitchell was able to manipulate or intimidate her.

Sophie's outfit for the day was described by fashion-conscious reporters:

> Black cashmere, buttoned down the back and [looking] as tho [sic] Sophia was poured into the model. Peeping from the collar at her neck…a baby blue cord, just enough of the color showing to add a chic appearance to the wearer. Her shoes are of patent leather with cloth tops and the skirt reaches to the top of her shoes. The only articles of jewelry which she wears are a plain band ring and a heart-shaped locket, which contains a picture of her mother and sister. The locket is suspended from her neck by a gold chain.[150]

Sophie was nervous and blamed her discomfort on the great number of women piling into the courtroom. "[I]t is the women who crowd in here and those that stand up that annoy me because I know they are looking at me all the time and I can't help being nervous."[151] Reporters noted than when Sophie became morose or nervous she would stare at the floor or fix her eyes "on the tip of her tiny shoe."[152] Lawyer Cassidy had objected to the presence of these women in court. There were at least seventy-five. Deputy Thomas J. O'Brian attempted to remove some of them, but they cast "caustic glances" at him and refused to budge.

Because of her condition of nervousness, Sophie would not testify this day. "When her counsel asked her if she was ready to go on the stand, she said, 'No, no.' She further explained, 'I intended to go on the stand this afternoon, but the sight of that large crowd in the court room scared me.' She added, 'I am not afraid of the jury or of the lawyers, but I do not like to have a crowd of women looking at me. My new dress does not fit me as well as I would like and women notice such things. When a woman is in trouble it is her own sex who gloat over the fact.'"[153]

In addition to the crowd of seemingly hostile female spectators, there were several medical experts and *alienists* (neurologists or psychiatrists—the fields overlapped in that day). They had been hired by both sides. Still to come would be a battle of the experts and the question of the admissibility of Walsh's transcript of the Q&A at the hospital.

The defense had procured the services of Dr. A.F. Diefendorf, who had been an expert for the prosecution in the famous *Thaw* case in New York City.[154] The other defense witnesses were Dr. Austin E. May (who practiced at 376 North Main in Union City) and Medical Examiner Dr. E.H. Johnson of Naugatuck. On the prosecution side were Dr. A.C. Thomas and Dr. Edwin Down, both noted authorities on insanity. The alienists for the state were as of yet unable to make any observations of her upon which to base such testimony if called.

From the defense's opening, it was clear that there was not going to be any claim of insanity. The theory the defense lawyers wanted to lay before the jury was that Sophia was of the personality type which allowed her to be led to do what Mitchell wanted her to do—that she was compelled to obey his orders.[155] Kennedy attempted to introduce a certificate showing that Sophie's half sister had died in 1904 after ingesting Paris green and that the secondary cause of her death was listed as insanity. Judge Curtis ruled this out in the absence of evidence that Sophie had ever been or was now insane.[156]

Kennedy pressed on and called Mrs. Mary Murphy of Union City to the stand. She testified that she had seen a person whom she was now able to identify as Joe Mitchell passing through the backyard of her house on Crown Street on Saturday morning. The man was walking toward the Golf Links, with Sophie in the lead. She had been shown a photo of Mitchell at police headquarters on September 20.

Mrs. Murphy's testimony was followed by that of Mrs. Petronia Petrupkalkis, who lived over the saloon owned by Ben Kulvinskas. She said that while she was picking mushrooms on Friday, September 17, she saw Sophie walking toward the place where Ben was found and that a man who was not Ben was walking in the same direction. Mrs. Petrupkalkis said that as he drew near her, the man covered his face with a handkerchief.

Victoria Zinkiene then testified that she saw a man who was not Ben walking toward the scene of the crime on September 17, but Zinkiene was described as "troubled with a failing memory."[157]

Then Henry Herman of Naugatuck claimed that he had had a conversation with Joseph Raytkiewich in which Raytkiewich told Herman that Ben had said, "Sofie [sic] Kritchman and Joe Mitchell shot me." This was in direct contradiction to Raytkiewich's earlier testimony that Ben had never mentioned Joe Mitchell.[158]

The defense also made some apparent headway tying the murder weapon to Mitchell, when Kennedy elicited from the detectives in the case that they had found a key in Mitchell's pocket that fit Antone Kulvinskas's trunk. This was the trunk which had housed the revolver that had been found near Ben's body—the revolver that Antone had testified had been stolen.

The defense then attempted to put Sophie on the stand, without being sworn, for the limited purpose of demonstrating that she was not strong enough to work the revolver used to shoot Ben.[159] No doubt the prosecution's thinking was that Sophie was not under oath, and even if she had been sworn she could fake her difficulty, and it would be problematic to cross-examine her effectively.[160] Judge Curtis sustained the prosecution's objection to such a "demonstration."

In addition to producing a series of witnesses who seemed to help Sophie emphasize Mitchell's role, the defense called a firearms expert, John E. Bassett, to testify as to his experiments standing at various distances and shooting at white cloth. The purpose of these experiments was to show that when he stood at twelve feet or more from the cloth when shooting, any powder marks were very faint or were absent. The defense was able to get into evidence the pieces of cloth used in Bassett's experiments. The suggestion was that someone other than Sophie—someone more distant from the victim—might have been the shooter. Kennedy also asked Bassett if he had not witnessed Sophie handling Exhibit 3—the pistol found at the crime scene—and whether she was able to make the cylinder revolve by pulling the trigger double-action style. Kennedy was trying to circumvent the judge's prior ruling on the point, but he was not successful. Kellogg's objection to the question was sustained.

Bassett was followed by Elizabeth Dullard, another local, who testified that she saw Sophie and a man who looked like a photograph of Joe Mitchell going toward Spring Street at about ten or eleven in the morning.[161]

Dr. Johnson, the medical examiner, was used to attack the reliability of the dying declarations. He testified that when he was called into the woods to the victim's side, Ben was "in no condition to make a statement. All his words were incoherent, and he was bordering on delirium. I did not pay any attention to his statements. I was unable to get one word of intelligence from him." He further stated that he telephoned Dr. Crane, the attending physician, and told him that "[i]t was impossible to get any statement from him which could be relied upon."

Cassidy then propounded a lengthy hypothetical question for the doctor to respond to (presumably for rhetorical purposes—a sort of argument or summation in the form of a question), but the judge adjourned for the day.[162] The lengthy hypothetical question had apparently come as something of a surprise to Prosecutor Kellogg, and he was probably grateful for the adjournment.

At some point Judge Curtis had issued an order excluding persons "not having business in the court," and this apparently calmed Sophie.

She said, "I am very thankful to Judge Curtis for keeping out those women who annoy me. They come in here just to look at me and they look at me and I cannot help catching their glances. I felt more comfortable this afternoon, and tonight I feel happy."[163]

Now the fight would turn to the Q&A statement (the Walsh Transcript) transcribed by clerk Thomas Walsh at the hospital in the presence of

Drs. Crane, Pomeroy, and Lawlor, along with Assistant Prosecutor McGrath, and then sworn to before Deputy Coroner Makepeace. The experts would disagree as to whether it was the product of a rational mind or an incoherent statement elicited by leading questions from a state "bordering on delirium."

Another issue was whether there was sufficient evidence that Ben had personal—or firsthand—knowledge of Mitchell's participation in the crime. Was he relying only on what Sophie had said at the scene?

In the absence of a transcript of the first trial, it is difficult to determine, based on the news reporting, when the Walsh Transcript was admitted. But the coverage of the second trial confirmed that it had been admitted during the prosecution's case in chief in the first one.[164]

Although the Walsh Transcript as it appeared word for word in the *Waterbury Republican*[165] is lengthy and perhaps a bit tedious, it is included below so that all readers can assess it for themselves.

Examined by Mr. Makepeace:

Dr. Crane: The doctors think there is no chance for you to get better. You are surely going to die, and the statement you make to these men you want to tell them knowing you are going to die and there is no chance for you to get well.

Q: Do you think you are going to get well?

A: I don't think so.

Q: Do you think you are going to get well?

A: I could not say.

Dr. Crane: You have got such a bad wound there is no chance for you to get well. You are surely going to die. We have given you every chance, and now you want to talk to these men understanding you are not going to get well. Do you understand me?
Witness: Yes. Sure.

Q: Do you believe what the doctor has just told you?

A: Sure.

Q: You do not think you are going to get well?

A: No.

Q: And you have sworn to speak the truth to what I am about to ask you?

A: Sure.

Q: Who shot you?

A: She shot me the first time. I am going to die.

Q: Did she shoot you the first time?

A: Yes, she shoot me.

Q: What is her name?

A: Sophia Kritchman.

Q: Where did she shoot you?

A: Just in the legs. I can't walk after that. I stay there on the outside. She is cut my neck already, and I—

Q: What day was this?

A: Just about Friday.

Q: What time of day?

A: I can't tell sure—about three o'clock, I guess.

Q: Where were you?

A: She said "Three funerals." She said. I said "Why?" "I shoot you and Joe Mitchell and myself and all die."

Q: I shoot you and I shoot Joe Mitchell?

A: Yes. Sure.

Q: And she shot you?

A: Yes.

Q: And she shot you? How many times?

A: Oh, GOD! Wait awhile. One time Friday and about three times on Saturday.

Q: What time Saturday?

A: About half past seven.

Q: In the morning?

A: Sure, in the morning.

Q: Where were you when she shot you the first time on Friday? Were you at home or in the business?

A: No, I was not at home. I was going to walk and she shoot me.

Q: Where did she shoot you? In the leg?

A: Yes, first time in leg; the second time she shoot me in the side.

Q: And the third time, where did she shoot you?

A: The third time she shoot me she look I going to be dead or not. "If you not be dead I will go and shoot you myself and Joe Mitchell too," she said.

Q: What time was that? On Saturday?

A: Yes.

Q: Where were you between the first time she shot you and the second time she shot you? Where did you stay?

A: I walked outside.

Q: Outside of your house?

A: Yes.

Q: Where did you stay after she shot you the second time?

A: I stayed there too.

Q: Did Joe Mitchell shoot you at all?

A: Yes, I think; I can't tell about sure.

Q: You didn't see him?

A: Sure. She says "Shoot him."

Q: Did you hear him talking with her?

A: Yes.

Q: What did he say?

A: She says "I walk around I was at three funerals." She says "First die me, another Joe Mitchell."

Q: What did Joe say? Joe was there the second time? You hear her talking with him the second time?

A: No, didn't talk. She says "There was three funerals this afternoon." I told her "What funerals?" "You first, Joe second, and I am third."

Q: Who cut your throat? Who cut your neck?

A: It was the girl.

Q: When did she do that?

A: She is not the first time. She says "I got a good wrist."

Q: When did she cut your throat? Friday.

Q: When did she first shoot you?

A: The first time. The first time she shot me.

Q: Did she cut your throat before she shot you or after?

A: After.

Q: What did she cut it with? Use a knife?

A: Yes, the same knife. Started to shot my legs. She says "I am going to shoot you." I told her "Why?" She says "It will be three funerals."

Q: That was Friday?

A: Yes. I told her "You will get no chance." After that I says "Let it go."

Q: When did she shoot you the last time?

A: Thursday—no. It was Saturday.

Q: What time in the day?

A: About in the afternoon—about three o'clock or four o'clock Friday.

Q: Your throat was cut on Friday?

A: Yes, Thursday,

Q: She shot you the first time. Now, let us be sure that we get this straight. First she shot you in the leg on Friday?

A: Yes. Started to fight and she shot me in the leg. I can't walk no more and can't fight.

Q: And she cut your throat?

A: Yes.

Q: That same time? On Thursday?

A: No Friday.

Q: Yesterday?

A: Yes.

Q: Yesterday she shot you the first time?

A: Yes.

Q: When did she shoot you the second time? The same day?

A: No. She says like that "Tonight would be funerals, three funerals. I cut your head off and Joe Mitchell's." "All right, let it go."

Q: When was the last time she shot you?

A: The last time?

Q: Yes. Yesterday?

A: Yesterday.

Q: And the day before yesterday was the first time?

A: Yes.

Q: Where did you stay?

A: In the saloon.

Q: Where did you stay after she cut your throat? Where did you stay?

A: Joe Mitchell.

Q: Where did you stay? Where were you? In the bushes?

A: Yes.

Q: Where? On the road?

A: About over a mile. As far as about over a mile.

Q: From where?

A: In the bushes.

Q: And you stayed there all night? Where did you stay all night?

A: Can't get no chance up to twelve o'clock.

Q: Where did you stay over night? You were in the bushes when she shot you the first time?

A: Yes.

Q: Where did you stay overnight? You were in the bushes when she shot you the second time?

A: Oh, the second time? In the bushes.

Q: Were you there all the time?

A: Yes.

Q: Were you just lying there?

A: Yes.

Q: You couldn't move?

A: Yes.

Q: What was the trouble about?

A: I don't know nothing about it.

Q: How long have you known her?

A: She says "Start to work in saloon make a little trouble." I say "What trouble?" She says "You have got lots of money," she says, "An I have got no much money." And laughing she says she says "I take some another fellow; nice fellow."

Q: Had you been going with her?

A: No.

Q: How long had she been your girl?

A: Mine? Oh, gosh! Just two times. I walk out with her.

Q: When were those two times? Just before this?

A: Yes.

Q: What was the trouble with Joe Mitchell?

A: She says she like him; he was a young fellow, a nice fellow, too. That is what she says. She says she don't care about the money; she like nice fellow. He get a little trouble. He was with another girl. Stay a little while and go back to the other girl. She told me "Oh, gosh! My fellow going away. I have to get another fellow."

Q: Did she tell Joe Mitchell that?

A: Yes.

Q: She has got another fellow?

A: Yes.

Q: She meant you?

A: Sure. Yes. "He is a nice looking fellow. I have another fellow." He fight about five or six times.

Q: She had five or six fellows?

A: No. She says she "couldn't get another fellow." That is what she said.

Q: You boarded with her mother, did you?

A: Yes.

Q: What did she have against you?

A: I don't know. She told me "very nice looking fellow she has got but he has no money the other fellow. He is a nice fellow." And then she say "Oh, Jesus I don't want to work for him."

Q: What did you tell her?

A: Her mother say to me "Why don't you keep that girl?" I say "I don't want for good." Her mother said "Joe has got the money." I have got a good girl. Oh, the girl good girl.

Q: When was this? The day before?

A: Yes.

Q: Did the girl say anything to you then?

A: No.

Q: She didn't say anything to you?

A: No.

Q: Did you tell her mother you didn't want her?

A: Yes.

Q: Did her mother tell her?

A: Sure.

Q: She told her that night?

A: Yes.

Q: And it was the next day she shot you?

A: Yes.

Q: Where did she work?

A: She didn't work. She played the piano very good. No work at all.

Q: Did she stay around the house?

A: Yes.

Q: Was she a good girl?

A: She was all right.

Q: Did you ever have anything to do with her?

A: No.

Q: Did Joe Mitchell?

A: Yes.

Q: Did you catch them together?

A: Sure. One day, I can't tell, one day she was with another girl already and she says "You have got no money Joe," Joe said "I have got money. Let her go."

Q: They were together?

A: Yes.

Q: You saw them together?

A: Yes.

Q: What did you say to her? She was your girl, wasn't she?

A: Let her go.

Q: Did you say "Let her go?"

A: Joe Mitchell.

Q: Did you ever have any quarrel with Joe Mitchell about her?

A: No.

Q: Did you talk with him about her?

A: I talked about making trouble.

Q: You told him it was making trouble?

A: Yes. He was drinking and I says "Where is the money?" He says "Let it go in the trust."

Q: The night before she shot you you had a talk with her mother?

A: Yes.

Q: And you said you didn't want her?

A: Yes.

Q: Did she come around to see you the next day?

A: Yes.

Q: What time did she come?

A: About five o'clock in the afternoon.

Q: She was around the house?

A: Yes

Q: Did you go out and walk with her?

A: I didn't walk with her then.

Q: Did you go up in the bushes?

A: Yes.

Q: How did you happen to meet her up there? Did she see you going up there or you see her going?

A: She going.

Q: You saw her going?

A: Yes.

Q: Did you speak to her?

A: Yes.

Q: What did you say?

A: I sais [sic] "That's a good girl. Don't be afraid. We are going to get married."

Q: And what did she say?

A: She said "All right my little boy."

Q: How long were you talking there together?

A: Oh, a little while. About a half hour or a little more. It was some time.

Q: Did you know she had a gun or revolver?

A: No, I didn't know anything about a gun.

Q: Did you see her pull out the gun?

A: No.

Q: What was the first thing you knew, when you was shot?

A: Ye[s].

Q: She shot you?

A: Yes.

Q: Did you see her shoot you?

A: No. She shot all right.

Q: How did you know she shot?

A: Oh, gosh! So many times.

Q: Did you see her shoot any of the time?

A: Sure.

Q: How many times did she hit you the first time that day?

A: About six times. Two times for twenty cents and the next time for twenty-five.

Q: Where did she hit you? In the legs?

A: Yes, in the legs. She hit me the next time in the head. Big lump in the back.

Q: Where did she hit you the first time.

A: At the cap.

Q: On the head?

A: Yes.

Q: Where did she shoot you the second time?

A: I can't tell you.

Q: The shot that hit the cap did not hit you?

A: Yes, the second time.

Q: It hit you?

A: Yes, the second time.

Q: Did you have your back turned towards her, or were you looking at her when she hit you?

A: Yes, sure.

Q: You saw her hit you?

A: She says "That's a good fellow." I said "Let her go."

Q: Did you see she had a gun.

A: Gun.

Q: Yes?

A: Sure, a revolver.

Q: And you said "Let it go?"

A: Sure.

Q: Did you know she was going to shoot you?

A: No. I am satisfied to get a good glass of whiskey.

There were things in the Walsh Transcript that could be used by both the defense and the prosecution. The defense could argue that the leading nature of questions put to Ben—and some of his odd answers—suggested the unreliability of the overall statement. Some of the details may also have suggested that the killing of Ben was part of Sophie's plan to kill both Ben and Joe Mitchell and then kill herself.

As the trial started up again, Kennedy called Captain Dodds (formerly Lieutenant Dodds][166] to the stand. Dodds testified that the key he took from Mitchell could open Antone's trunk. Kennedy also got a concession from Antone that he had conversed with Raytkiewich before the trial had opened—perhaps suggesting that the two were out to get Sophie? The defense then called Edward O'Brien, who said that he was present at the scene of the crime and that he had not heard Ben make any statement.[167]

Kennedy called Mrs. Kate Melowski, who denied that she had told the grand jury that she saw Mitchell at the Kritchman home on the day of the shooting; but she did concede that she knew Raytkiewich and had talked to him about the case.

Then eleven-year-old Mamie Kritchman testified that she had seen Mitchell many times at the Kritchman home and that she had seen him lying on the bed in the room occupied by Antone Kulvinskas.

Next Charles Baxter was called to testify that he saw Raytkiewich at the crime scene, but he, too, had not heard the victim say anything. Sophie's defense team seemed to be scoring points, raising doubts about the dying declarations that implicated Sophie, while stacking up evidence against Mitchell. Kennedy turned things over to his junior counsel, Cassidy.

Cassidy again put his twelve-hundred-word hypothetical question to veteran Medical Examiner Dr. Johnson, who was of the opinion that Ben was not of sound mind when he was questioned at length at the hospital. This time Prosecutor Kellogg was prepared for the hypothetical question and the doctor's opinion. It was said that Dr. Johnson was given "the stiffest cross-examination that [had] ever been given to a witness in a court of law in Waterbury" but that the doctor held up before the onslaught. His testimony contradicted that of Dr. Crane that

Ben was able to make a dying declaration. Cassidy also argued that the questions given to Ben were leading and suggestive. It was now clear that the alienists summoned by the state were in the wings to shore up Dr. Crane's assessment—not to testify as to Sophie's sanity.[168]

MISTRIAL

When the third week of the trial opened on February 8, 1910, it was anticipated that the defense would call Dr. Allen R. Diefendorf of New Haven and Dr. Austin E. May of Naugatuck to give their opinions regarding Ben's inability to make a reliable dying declaration. They would be cross-examined by Prosecutor Kellogg. Then Sophie would tell her story. Counting all the witnesses, the trial was expected to go on for at least another week.

Before the defense continued with its case, there would be a touch of drama. The regular guards, Deputy Sheriff Farrel (of New Haven) and Thomas J. O'Brian, were joined by Deputy Sheriff Theodore F. Wheeler. It was reported that Wheeler was known "for his aggressiveness and

Deputy Sheriff Theodore F. Wheeler (22)

ability to discern the intention of any person who would attempt to do any untoward act."[169]

Kennedy had made arrangements for Deputy Sheriff Wheeler to join the other two sheriffs after Kennedy's junior counsel, Cassidy, had received a letter dated February 4, 1910, written in Lithuanian and mailed to the courthouse. The letter threatened Sophie's death if she testified against Mitchell.

> I am very sorry for you, but I have to shoot you. If I don't shoot you, then they will shoot me. You have two days yet to live, after that I will have to kill you. Tell that you killed Kulvinskas, then we don't do nothing to you, but if you are going to say that Peeziulis [sic] killed him, then I will have to shoot you. Take all the fault on yourself, after that we will help you, if not do not forget I will have to shoot you and kill you. Kulvinskas promised us he would not say that he was killed differently, you have to say that you Sofe [sic] Kritchman have killed him. We will watch you every day and you will not live very long.[170]

The letter was not signed, but it was reported that it bore a bloodstain at the bottom.[171] Had it actually been sent by Mitchell's supporters? This would shore up Kennedy's conspiracy theory. Or was it a ploy from Sophie's side?

The letter had been published in the papers that very morning. Prosecutor Kellogg faced a difficult choice. If he requested an *admonition*—a direction by the court that the jury disregard the contents of the letter and any newspaper coverage they had been exposed to—it might only emphasize the matter in the minds of the jurors. Arguing that Kennedy had given the letter to the press, Kellogg moved for a mistrial and the discharge of the jury.

Judge Curtis granted Kellogg's motion.[172] The judge expressed shock that the newspapers had printed the contents of the letter for all to see, citing a 1908 opinion of the Connecticut Supreme Court condemning similar publications, and urged Kellogg to bring charges against any offending newspapers.[173]

Judge Curtis also reprimanded Kennedy and dismissed him as state-ap-pointed counsel for Sophia Kritchman, although that would not prevent Kennedy from appearing in future proceedings if he were retained and paid by the Kritchman family. He was so retained in short order.[174]

A false rumor circulated in some circles that Kennedy had been disbarred.[175] In his own defense, Kennedy tried to explain that a reporter had somehow "been apprised in some way or other of [the letter's] contents and asked us for it, and in order to do away with unfounded speculations, and in order to get matters straight in the press, we gave the letter to the reporter."[176] Was Kennedy trying to get inadmissible evidence to the jury through the back door—through the media of the day? The message to the jury was that his client was in danger. There was a plot against her by Mitchell's supporters. Some of the prosecution's witnesses were part of the plot. She should be believed. They should not be believed. Presumably the appearance of Deputy Sheriff Wheeler was part of the theater. If this had been the plan, it all turned out to be a big mistake.

The next thing Kennedy did was file a motion for dismissal of the case against Sophie on grounds that *jeopardy had attached*—that a new trial was barred by the rule against double jeopardy.[177] Kennedy argued that the mistrial had been granted at the request of the prosecution and that the discharge of the jury had been unnecessary.[178] She could not be tried again.

Kellogg put the blame on the defense for releasing the letter to the press. A renewed motion for a mistrial was denied in due course by Judge William H. Williams,[179] who would set the case for retrial and replace Judge Curtis as the presiding judge.[180] A trial judge has discretion to declare a mistrial even over the defendant's objection if there is a "manifest necessity" to do so. Judge Williams showed by his ruling that he thought that Judge Curtis had been justified in doing so and that the defense should not benefit from Judge Curtis's ruling.

Now the case took an important turn. There was a curious letter in the Records of the Superior Court from Judge Curtis to State's Attorney Kellogg, dated February 9, 1910. Although it is difficult to read, the gist of it seems to be that Judge Curtis was having second thoughts about whether he should have granted a separate trial for Sophie in the first place. He was aware that Kellogg was renewing a request for a joint trial,

Stratford
Feby. 9/10

Dear Mr Kellogg:

In reference to the motion which you state you propose to make for a joint trial of Sophie Krilchman and Mitchell, I wish to relieve the court from feeling bound to follow my ruling. Before passing upon that question I read the Coroner's notes through. If the signed declaration of Krilowskas and the testimony of the woman who was at work on the golf links had been included in those notes I should undoubtedly have denied the motion for separate trials.

You may use this note before the court if you so desire.

Yours Very Tly
H.H. Curtis

Letter February 9, 1910, from Judge Howard Curtis to John P. Kellogg (23)

which would give the advantage back to the prosecution—the defendants would attack each other. Judge Curtis did not want Judge Williams to feel bound by his earlier ruling granting separate trials. He asked that Kellogg show the letter to Judge Williams if he so desired. Was that proper?

Kellogg moved for a joint trial, and in a hearing on the matter before Judge Williams, he cited Judge Curtis's letter. The lawyers for both defendants—Sophie and Mitchell—strongly opposed the motion.[181] Judge Williams decided that this time there would be a joint trial of both defendants. Kennedy filed a formal objection to the impaneling of a new jury, complaining that Judge Curtis had been correct in granting separate trials because Sophie's "defense and interests conflicted with those of Mitchell [and] that she could not get a fair and impartial trial jointly with said Mitchell,"[182] but to no avail.

Presumably the prosecution hoped that a joint trial would result in a "cutthroat defense," with each defendant trying to prove that the other did the deed.[183] Strictly speaking, this case was a bit different because there was only one cutthroat, and that was Sophie (no pun intended). That is, it appeared—at this point, at least—that Joe Mitchell was not trying to shift blame in the same way that Sophie was. He had not turned state's evidence, and all along he had contended that he was "not there" and that he knew nothing about the crime. He had an alibi. Perhaps this is a fine point. In any event, the trial judge did not seem to grasp it and ruled in favor of a joint trial on the theory that there was evidence that Sophie and Mitchell had been in cahoots—that there had been a conspiracy to kill Ben.

Judge Williams repeated Judge Curtis's warning against publications that might interfere with a new trial, citing *State v. Howell*, the case that Judge Curtis had alluded to in granting Kellogg's motion for a mistrial.[184] The show was starting all over.

PART THREE

Joint Trial

Joint Trial Opens

Sophie Kritchman, the Union City piano teacher, and Joe Mitchell, her alleged lover and accomplice, were seated at the same table in the courtroom on February 15, 1910, before presiding Judge William H. Williams as jury selection for their joint trial—the second trial for Sophie—began. When the first panel of fifty was exhausted with only five jurors seated, a second panel had to be summoned. Selection continued to be challenging because "practically all the men examined declared they had been prejudiced" by newspaper accounts of Sophie's first trial. Once again Sophie took an active part, insisting that her lawyers consult her, and on occasion she "whispered into their ear," which appeared to "annoy" Kennedy "as a frown passed over his face each time."

Mitchell "seemed to take little interest" in the process.[185] The selection of twelve jurors dragged on and took most of four days, the lawyers going through almost two hundred talesmen.[186] On the third day, February 17, Judge Williams, upon the suggestion of the sheriff, permitted Mitchell to "be kept constantly" in "an improvised cell" in the courthouse until the end of the trial because of the size of the crowds showing interest in him. One newspaper reported that "[fully] 3,000 'morbidly curious,' a majority being women and small children, followed Mitchell from the New Haven trolley car to the very steps of the courthouse, chattering excitedly and passing remarks about the prisoner."[187] As jury selection neared its end, Mitchell's demeanor changed from disinterest and glumness. A "smile actually illuminated his features.… [I]t is understood that he 'cheered up' on advice of his counsel, who realized that jurymen, being only human, are no more fond of sulkers than are most responsible citizens."[188]

For the fashion conscious, Sophie was dressed differently. "She wore a white lawn waist with a black shirt. She also wore a Buster Brown collar which gave her a more youthful appearance than ever."[189]

Prosecutor Kellogg warned reporters that he would bring legal proceedings against any newspaper or reporter who violated the law. This sent the newspaper men scurrying to Judge Williams for guidance, but the judge was "not committal."[190]

As the trial opened on February 18, 1911, arguments resumed over the dying declarations and the admissibility of the victim's "blood stained and bullet riddled...apparel." As Dr. Crane examined Ben's bloodstained shirt and "wrapper," a bullet that had not been seen before dropped out of it and fell onto the floor, presumably to the horror of some and the amusement of others.[191] The clothing was admitted over defense objections.[192]

There had been a break in the action on February 22 due to the illness of one of the jurors,[193] after which the trial proceeded on February 28 much as before, with a great deal of evidence and argument outside the presence of the jury[194] as to the dying declarations, to determine their admissibility. If—and when—the statements were admitted, the jury would hear most of the same arguments because they bore on the weight to be given them. Judge Williams was of the opinion that there was no doubt that Ben knew he was near death and had no hope of recovery.[195]

There was a second disruption of the proceedings when the trial had to be moved from the Waterbury Courthouse to New Haven because contractors who were to build a new structure demanded that the Waterbury building be turned over to them.[196] When it came time for the prisoners to be taken to the jail in New Haven, Sophie refused to ride in the same car with Mitchell.[197] The new venue did not please Sophie, because the large crowds, which even filled the galleries, made her nervous. Previously reported to be "pleased at the prospect of having court sit in New Haven," Sophie now "regretfully" observed, "I prefer a smaller crowd."[198]

Available newspaper copy of the second trial is comparatively spotty, but it seems like the trial played out pretty much the same way this time, with the same witnesses. Judge Williams admitted into evidence the short dying declaration taken by Assistant Prosecutor McGrath and witnessed by Dr. Crane,[199] over Kennedy's objection.[200]

Streetcar conductor Patrick Monahan testified that he saw Sophie and Mitchell on his car, but he could not remember whether this was on Friday or Saturday.[201] His testimony seemed shaky.[202] Frank Nolan of the *Naugatuck Daily News* would later testify that he was on a trolley car going from Waterbury to Naugatuck on Saturday morning, September 18, 1909, and that he saw Sophie on the car but not Mitchell.[203]

Victoria Dalton's testimony included something new this time around.[204] In the first trial she had identified a pair of garters that Sophie was having trouble with when she and Sophie were on their walk. This time Victoria told the same story of having gone with Sophie to the clump of bushes (near the victim) and of having heard a voice call, "Sophie, Sophie," "Police, Police," and "Antone, oh, Antone."

Victoria testified, "When Sophie came out of the bushes I asked her who it was, and she said 'a tramp.' She then asked me to find a stone and she would throw it into the bushes. I went down on both knees, put up my hands and begged her to come home…We walked as far as Mr. Booth's garden, where Sophie had trouble with her stocking…she took something long, black and shiny from her stocking. Then she put it back again. I gave her my hair ribbon and she tied up the stocking, then she went home.

"Did Sophie say anything more to you?" asked Prosecutor Arnold A. Alling.

Victoria replied, "Yes, just before we got to my house she told me not to tell my mother that I heard any hollering because we would be arrested and have to go to court and I would never see my mother again."

Prosecutor Alling continued, "Did you hear Sophie say, 'If you come near me I will kill you?'"

Victoria replied, "No. I just heard the man say 'Sophie, Sophie,' 'Police, Police,' and, 'Antone, oh, Antone.' Then I heard someone say, 'Shut up, or I'll kill you.'"[205]

The witness said that at the time she never heard the name Mitchell mentioned.

Taking up a pair of garters, defense counsel Kennedy asked, "Isn't this what you said Sophie took from her stocking?"

Victoria replied, "No sir." [breaking down and crying]

She explained that she was frightened in the first trial and didn't know what to say. Kennedy reminded her of her former testimony, reading from the transcript. The child stuck to her guns, insisting that what Sophie took from her stocking was "long, black, and shiny." She said that she understood what she had said in the first trial but that it was not right and she wanted "this time to tell what was right." On redirect Prosecutor Alling asked why she had told Kennedy only about the garters in the first trial. She answered, "[Kennedy] had frightened me."[206] Her testimony now was consistent with what she had told the police early in the investigation.[207]

Victoria's testimony was followed by that of Antone Kulvinskas, who testified that the key found on Mitchell opened the trunk in which Antone had kept his revolver.[208] Louis Schneer, the pawnbroker's clerk, again testified as to Sophie's purchase of a pistol for three dollars. On cross-examination he agreed that she had not pulled the trigger, but on redirect he said that she had pulled back the hammer. However, when the weapon was introduced, the court struck out any answers as to what Sophie did with the weapon, at the prosecutor's request. Kennedy excepted.

John Mates, the doorman at the Waterbury police station, testified that he found a bunch of keys on Mitchell and that he opened Antone's trunk with one. The trunk was then offered into evidence. Mrs. Kate Sodolosky testified to having lent Sophie five dollars for car fare on Saturday morning. Mrs. Dalton, Victoria's mother, testified how Sophie came home with Victoria on the evening of September 17. She saw Sophie leave her house between one and two o'clock on Friday afternoon and that Ben left ten minutes later. When Sophie returned between five and six o'clock, Ben was not with her. Later Sophie took a walk and returned home before seven o'clock for supper.

Michael Narayacks, a friend of Antone, testified that on the Sunday before the killing, he gave Antone two razors but that when he asked for their return after the killing, he was told that one of them could not be found.[209] This testimony had not been offered in the first trial or during the coroner's investigation.[210] Kennedy would intimate that the testimony about the razors had been concocted to back up Victoria's new testimony.

Nellie Sodolosky, a friend of Sophie, testified that when she took a walk with Sophie on Friday night, Sophie had told her that she was going to marry Joe Mitchell. Annie Hessenger testified that she saw Sophie and Victoria walk by her house going toward Union City and that she saw Sophie the next morning, which was Saturday, walking up Spring Street in the direction of Union City. Then came Mary Petrukatis (previously referred to as Mrs. Petronia Petrupkalkis), who lived over Ben Kulvinskas's saloon. Again, she said that Friday afternoon, about one o'clock, after she had been picking mushrooms in Wilmot's Woods (probably near 173 Spring Street, where a Wilmot family lived), she came out onto Spring Street near McDermott's farm and saw a man walking rapidly along the road. Ten minutes later she heard four shots coming from an area where Ben was found. On cross-examination Kennedy brought out that Petrukatis did not think that the man she saw was Antone or Ben Kulvinskas because if it had been one of them the man probably would have talked to her or acknowledged her in some way.[211]

On March 4, 1910, Judge Williams ruled out some of the statements that Ben had supposedly made to his friends, but then he admitted the bloodstained note that Judge Curtis had excluded in the first trial.[212]

By March 7, the prosecution was beginning to wind up its case with the testimony of two of its most important witnesses—Police Chief Schmidt and Antone Kulvinskas.

Chief Schmidt testified that when he suggested to Antone that Ben may have tried to commit suicide, the wounded man turned his head toward Chief Schmidt and said, "No. No. Sophia Kritchman and Joe Mitchell killed me and Sophia Kritchman cut my neck."[213]

Kennedy did score some points on cross, getting the chief to say, "I don't remember," several times when asked about his testimony in the first trial. Judge Williams came to the witness's rescue by suggesting that it was not necessary to go over former testimony unless it was inconsistent, suggesting that Kennedy move along. However, Kennedy got the witness to testify that the victim's shirt and clothing were covered with blood and that there was a lot of blood on the grass. He then displayed the note "which show[ed] only a slight trace of blood." Kennedy was suggesting that Ben had not penned the note. Still, Chief Schmidt said that he had seen Antone pick up the note and the revolver when the chief made his second visit to the scene.[214] Was it possible that the note could have been planted after the chief's quick, first visit, while he was going for an ambulance?[215] But then why would Antone have planted it or not have seen someone plant it?

Again, Antone testified as to Ben's dying declarations:

As soon as I got there I said, "How did you come to be here" and he said "Sophia Kritchman brought me here and then shot me. She told me to take off my coat and lay down. Then she put a handkerchief over my face, telling me that it would keep the flies off my face. She said she would go out in the road to see if anyone was coming. She came back in half a minute and said, 'Why do you go with me and make trouble between myself and my man?' Then she shot me five times and threw the revolver at me."[216]

Repeating his testimony in the first trial, Antone said that his brother told him that he did not see Mitchell but heard his voice. He told of finding $196 in Ben's pocket, which was not consistent with Sophie's story that the original plan of the two was to rob him.[217]

On behalf of Mitchell, Attorney Lynch got Antone to repeat the victim's statement that Sophie had said she was going to kill herself.

Yes, he said Sophia told him that she was going to kill herself after she shot him and she said that there would be three funerals, a saloon keeper, a bartender and a piano player.[218]

Assistant Prosecutor McGrath followed with Ben's identification of Mitchell at the hospital as the man who shot him, along with Mitchell's response: "Christ Almighty, I didn't do this." McGrath also identified the bloody handkerchief, which was admitted in evidence. The prosecution offered Ben's bloody shirt and the bullet that had dropped out of it when it had been exhibited in court earlier in the trial.[219]

It is of interest that Prosecuting Attorney John M. Sweeney of Naugatuck testified that he had briefly gotten involved in the investigation on September 18 and was with the officers who found Sophie at home in the cellar. He said that when he placed his hand on her shoulder, she said, "I did not hurt Bronie."[220] If this statement was volunteered and not elicited by an accusation, it was telling.

Despite the fact that the press found all of this "clinching," Sophie smiled and shook her head, telling reporters, "I cannot help feeling happy. I do not fear perjury, and every word that was uttered by Antone Kulvinskas was far from the truth. He has perjured himself on the witness stand, and the truth will come out."[221]

At the end of its case Prosecutor Alling attempted to offer into evidence the bullet that had been found in Kulvinskas's clothing that had been shown to the jury in Waterbury before the case was transferred to New Haven. Judge Williams wanted evidence that it was of the same caliber as the revolver found near Kulvinskas's body. At this point Alling abruptly announced that the "State Rests," which surprised everyone.[222]

Sophie Tells Her Story

Now it was time for the defense to respond to the prosecution's array of incriminating facts. Kennedy was going to try to prove that Sophie was more a pawn than a participant. To do this he had to place Mitchell near the scene of the crime on Friday and Saturday and to emphasize that Mitchell had a motive—an axe to grind with Ben. The prosecution had offered some ineffectual testimony that streetcar conductor Monahan had let Joe Mitchell off at St. Mary Catholic church in Union City—but on which day, Friday or Saturday?[223]

Kennedy at this point called several witnesses to the stand to give testimony. Mrs. Mary Murphy was called to testify that she saw Sophie and Mitchell crossing her yard on Saturday morning, going in the direction of the Golf Links, which led to the crime scene. She was "positive."[224] Mrs. Murphy said that Mitchell had been in the lead. She added that she took particular notice because she had been told that Sophie was taking walks with young men. Naturally Mrs. Murphy was curious who the man might be.[225]

As to Mitchell's motive, Sophie's half sister, Nellie Antonaitis, testified that Mitchell and Ben quarreled over Sophie and the quarrel ended in a fight that spilled out into the Kritchman backyard.[226] On cross-examination Alling, for the prosecution (Kennedy and the prosecution were working hand in hand against Mitchell to provide a motive), alluded to Nellie's testimony before the coroner that something had happened between Sophie and Ben on Thursday—*that he may have assaulted her*. She had been acting strange, sometimes excited, and had indicated that she had been insulted in some way. Perhaps Sophie had told Mitchell of this?

There were other attempts to make a defense by way of blame-shifting, with Kennedy essentially serving as a second prosecutor. One example had to do with testimony elicited by Kennedy from Captain Dodds of the Waterbury Police Department Detective Bureau. Dodds said that streetcar conductor Monahan had reported (*hearsay objection, please?*) that Joe Mitchell had been on his car and had given a signal to stop at St. Mary church in Union City to meet with Sophie. He admitted that Monahan had not said which day this occurred. The idea was to put Mitchell in town when the crime was committed, to contradict an anticipated alibi defense.[227]

Kennedy called Drs. Pomeroy, Lawlor, and Johnson to testify on the subject of Ben's weak condition at the hospital. Again, the object of the exercise was to attack the reliability of Ben's statements made *in extremis*, which so thoroughly implicated Sophie. Dr. Johnson was emphatic that "from the amount of blood the man had lost, it would impair the accuracy of his statements." Kennedy also persisted in trying to get in evidence of Sophie's inability to pull the trigger of the weapon double-action style. Again, he was blocked by objections. Still, his arguments and comments got his point across to the jury.[228]

The most startling and damaging evidence against Mitchell came when a new witness, John Weisman of Union City, testified that he saw Mitchell on Anderson Street in Union City on Friday, September 17. Weisman said his identification was "positive," and he identified Mitchell in court. This would be a hard blow to Mitchell's alibi defense, and it corroborated Mrs. Murphy's testimony. It was reported that Weisman's testimony "came as a shock" to Mitchell's lawyers.[229] The prosecution had not called Weisman. He was someone Kennedy had come up with.

Lawyer Lynch, defense counsel for Mitchell, tried to impeach this important witness for bias, pointing out that Weisman's son was a lawyer who was helping Kennedy collect evidence for the defense. Kennedy bristled and for a moment the two lawyers squared off. This was something of a distraction, and Weisman never actually answered Lynch's accusatory question.[230] Needless to say, the prosecutors had no cross-examination for Weisman, whose testimony had helped them greatly.

At this point the Walsh Transcript was put into evidence—this time

Gaylord Farm Sanatorium, Wallingford, Connecticut, published by
L.R. Stimpson, Wallingford, Connecticut; postcard by The Albertype Co.,
Brooklyn, New York (24)

by Kennedy. It had been offered by Prosecutor Kellogg in the first trial, but the newspaper accounts do not mention him offering it in the second. Kennedy had apparently decided that the Walsh Transcript supported Dr. Johnson's testimony that Ben was *out of it*, to use a modern expression.

Lawyer Lynch scored some points for Mitchell by getting Makepeace to agree that two questions and answers were not in the record—specifically, "I asked him if he saw Joe Mitchell, and he answered 'No.' Then I asked him why he told me Joe Mitchell was there, if he did not see him, and he answered, 'Sophie told me.'"

Kennedy then called—as he had during the first trial—a local barber and Lithuanian interpreter, Joseph A. Shunskis, to give yet another translation of the "bloody note" that was more favorable to his client. With that the court adjourned for the day.[231]

The next day, March 10, 1910, Sophie took the stand. Kennedy began his direct examination of Sophie by taking her through the story of her life, including her education at the convent of the Sisters of the Holy Ghost, her jobs at the telephone exchange and in retail stores in Naugatuck, and her work, for a short time, as a boarder at the Gaylord Farm in Wallingford. (All present would have known that this was a tuberculosis sanatorium, which some years later would be the setting of Eugene O'Neill's play *The Straw*.)

Sophie recounted how she had studied music with the Sisters of Mercy in Naugatuck and told of her music pupils. She was uncertain of her age but guessed that it was somewhere between "not yet twenty" and twenty-four. She testified that she was engaged to Dr. A.K. Rutkauskas of Chicago, who would show up at the trial on March 14.[232] The good doctor gave an interview to the press and told reporters that he would marry Sophie if she were acquitted.[233] As to her other suitors, Sophie testified that she had never been engaged to Ben or Mitchell. She said that she had met Joe Mitchell when she was attending Monroe's Business College in Waterbury. Kennedy took her over the "attentions" paid to her by Ben and Mitchell at her home on Anderson Street and asked about their rivalry. Ben supposedly told her that "he could not live without" her and told of Mitchell's relationship with a married Lithuanian woman.[234] This led to the story of the fight between the two suitors in Sophie's backyard.[235]

Sophie then told the story of how she and Ben came to be at the crime scene. She claimed that Ben saw a man he believed to be Mitchell. She said that she and Ben went to the place between the bushes and an apple tree and sat down. At this point her testimony took a dramatic turn, as she broke down and told how Ben had made "improper proposals to her."[236]

He—told me to lie down and—then he…

[From the reporter] The rest of the story cannot be told but it was a thrilling tale of an attempted assault which failed of its intended purpose, according to the witness, and then she resumed:

I heard a noise and Ben jumped up. I heard a shot and then I heard more and they came out just as rapid as they could come. Ben said "Oh, Sophia," and I looked up and I saw Joe Mitchell. Then I screamed just as hard as I could scream and then ran out in the road. I saw Joe Mitchell and he had a revolver in his hand. He came up to me and caught me by the arm and he dragged me down the road. Then I said to him, "Joe, why did you shoot Ben?" and he told me to "shut up."

[After another crying fit, she continued.]

I ran until I was so weak I could not go any further. Then he came up to me and said: "He won't chase after you anymore." I said I didn't mind him chasing after me and why did you shoot him? Then he said "If you don't shut up, I will kill you," and I replied "No, Joe, I won't tell any one if you don't touch me." He told me to be sure to meet him on Bridge Street at a quarter to seven in the morning…."[237]

At this point the court was adjourned. Sophie would return to the stand later for cross-examination. She "staggered as she left the witness box," and taking a seat near her sister Nellie Antonaitis, she "went into a hysterical fit of weeping," which the jury witnessed as they were led from the courtroom. A reporter heard Mitchell whispering over and over, "Well, that's funny, that's funny," and he smiled as she wept.

The spectators seemed more impressed than her codefendant, as Sophie reported "all the nauseating details" of the supposed assault "in a tear laden voice":

[E]very spectator leaned forward and each glanced at the accused girl. The silence was intense, as Sophia talked in a low tone of voice which could be heard only when complete quiet prevailed in the room. Every syllable uttered by the girl in that recital of assault was absorbed as greedily and with as much abandon as is exhibited by a swarm of blue bottle flies feasting upon a putrid carcass.[238]

Of her seven hours total on the witness stand, five were spent under stiff cross-examination, during which her love letters to Mitchell were read. She "seemed to possess a strange infatuation" for him.[239] Judge Williams also allowed into evidence her testimony before the coroner, over the objection that the coroner had used "third degree" tactics on her, had kept her from her family, and had frightened her. The prior testimony contained many things inconsistent with her new story.

Still, Sophie's performance seemed to be judged as positive by some, and the formerly hostile females in the audience showered her with candy and flowers.[240] By this time the center section of the gallery of the courtroom had been taken over by Yale students, the "'rah, rah' boys," who "[did] not hesitate to espouse her cause whenever her name [was] mentioned."[241]

Others were skeptical. The *Waterbury Republican* posed this question: "Is Sophie Kritchman the child that she appears to be on the witness stand, or is she a bright, intelligent young woman who is acting a part?"[242]

Sophie went on about her appointment with Mitchell on Spring Street road at six forty-five on Saturday morning. When he did not show up, she went to St. Mary church and "prayed for Ben." She claimed that she lost her money there and tried to borrow car fare from Mr. French. She accounted for her activities up to the time she met Victoria Dalton, claiming that she was in fear of being attacked by Mitchell. She said that she went with Victoria to see if she could be of assistance to Ben Kulvinskas, when she heard him say, "Who's there?" to which she answered, "Sophia." Then someone else said, in a man's voice, "Shut up, or I'll kill you." She fled through the bushes and broke a garter in the process and borrowed a ribbon from Victoria to tie up her stockings. She identified the garter handed to her by Kennedy as being the very one.[243]

Sophie said that she had never handled a revolver before until she bought one at the Waterbury pawn shop. She claimed that when she finally met Mitchell on Saturday, he had told her to buy the gun, which she turned over to him. He then forced her to go where Ben lay. She said that she went into the bushes, and she heard five or six shots.[244]

At this point Kennedy handed her Exhibit 21—the revolver—which she identified. She said she could not pull the trigger, and Kennedy again asked her to demonstrate.[245] Although she was under oath this time, the court would not allow such a demonstration, presumably because her performance could be *self-serving* (faked). Because Sophie had become fatigued, court was adjourned for the day. Her defense was nearing its conclusion.

One wonders whether the jurors noticed some weaknesses in Sophie's testimony. During her cross-examination Kellogg held up a bloodstained handkerchief before her, lifting it by one corner. Sophie denied ever having seen it before.[246] Kellogg's point was that this was the handkerchief that she had put over the victim's face. On one corner of the handkerchief was the letter *K*. Was the jury to believe that Ben Kulvinskas carried monogrammed handkerchiefs? Kellogg also bore in with incredulity that she had worried about "Ben lying out there in the bushes all alone," while she said nothing, and that after she went to church to pray for Ben, she went to Waterbury to buy a revolver. Did the jury buy the new explanation she was now offering that she borrowed it to buy sheet music?[247]

The remainder of her defense would consist of the attacks of her expert witnesses on the various dying declarations of Ben. At this point the question was not the *admissibility* but the *reliability* of the evidence, which was a matter for the jury. Defense counsel Cassidy got to use his lengthy hypothetical question again, a mini-summation, to elicit opinion testimony that a man in Ben's condition could not have supplied accurate, coherent, reliable responses to the questions put to him at the time he gave the "so-called dying statement" at the hospital.[248]

The determined Kennedy tried one more time to get evidence in the record of Sophie's inability to pull the trigger double-action style. He tried to get it in through the *backdoor* by recalling John E. Bassett, the firearms expert. Bassett was allowed to testify that he witnessed Sophie pull the trigger "until the muscles in her arm were drawn taught and the blood[249] had settled at the ends of her fingers," but "she was unable to move the hammer a hair's breadth." He further testified that it would take twenty to twenty-five pounds of pressure to fire the weapon (if the hammer were not pulled back first). Bassett bore up under cross-examination by Prosecutor Alling. Kennedy had finally gotten in what he wanted in.[250]

Sophie's last witness was Dr. Rutkauskas, who had been with her all during the morning session and "seemed to be a great comfort to the prisoner."[251] He was questioned about his courtship by correspondence and about the couple's engagement. When Kennedy asked the doctor if they were engaged, a spectator rose and called out, "I object!" One assumes that this was a source of amusement as well as amazement.[252]

Now it was Joe Mitchell's turn.

Mitchell's Defense

As Mitchell's lawyers began his defense, a reporter for the *Waterbury Republican* made an astute observation:

> Attorney Kennedy of counsel for Miss Kritchman has proven himself to be an able assistant to attorneys for the state in dragging information from witnesses which has a tendency to connect Mitchell with the murder of Bronislaw Kulvinskas and the double cross-examination assists in causing delay.[253]

Mitchell's defense would consist of a parade of witnesses who would try to prove a negative—that he could not have been at the scene of the crime on September 16, 17, or 18—particularly Friday, September 17, and Saturday, September 18.[254] But as the reporters viewed it:

> The witnesses almost without exception were able to remember exactly what took place on the three days in question and when and where almost to a minute the place they saw Mitchell (at the saloon where he worked, for example), but on cross-examination it was difficult for them to recall when or where they had ever seen Mitchell and took refuge with an "I don't remember" answer.[255]

Does this mean that they were lying? Not necessarily, but lawyers worth their salt know that too many "I don't remember[s]" will discredit any witness.[256] All of this played into Kennedy's theory that there was a conspiracy to protect Mitchell.

The jury could not have missed the fact that almost all the witnesses were personal friends of Mitchell. "There was a sameness about the evidence given that verged on the monotonous."[257] Some of the testimony even drew some laughter—for example, when one witness answered in so low a voice that Judge Williams asked him if there was anything wrong with his lungs and when one witness said that he had seen Mitchell in saloons many times but did not care to say how many drinks he had seen him imbibe.[258]

On the other hand, Detective Thomas Colasanto testified that on a trip from Union City to Waterbury, Sophie told him that a man named Johnson shot Ben Kulvinskas. This testimony was replicated by a Detective Kennaugh, who said that on a trip from the hospital to the police station, Sophie told him that a man named John or Johnson did the shooting.[259] Coming from police witnesses, one would think that this information might have put some doubts in the jurors' minds.

Now Mitchell took the stand, and here is an object lesson for every suspect and every fledgling lawyer. When you are told not to talk, take that advice. Once you tell a story, you are stuck with it. When Mitchell was called before the coroner, he "locked his jaws and forgot the combination."[260] Because of that he could take the stand without being torn to pieces by prior inconsistent statements.

Of particular interest was Mitchell's testimony about his hospital conversation, in Lithuanian, with Ben.

> Bronislaw said in Lithuanian "Joe, didn't you shoot me from behind?" I said "Christ Almighty, I didn't do that." Bronislaw replied "Sophie told me."…Then I said "Bronislaw, I didn't see you or Sophia since Thursday night." He said, "I didn't see you, but Sophia told me."

Mitchell was on the stand for eleven and a half hours. During his direct examination, "he had accounted for nearly all the time on September 16, 17, and 18," but "when taxed with [some inconsistencies or] omissions, he 'did not remember.'"[261]

Kennedy hoped to prejudice the jury against Mitchell by boring in on his relationship with a widow, Mrs. Annie Bowers. The gist of it all was that he was keeping company with Mrs. Bowers and Sophie at the same time.[262] Nothing works like character assassination, if you can get away with it. Mitchell was embarrassed and evasive during the questioning.[263]

Kennedy ended his cross-examination by reading from the letters Sophie had sent Mitchell. Sophie blushed at some of the passages, and the women spectators "[l]eaned forward drinking in every word." Judge Williams threatened to clear the court if the laughter did not stop.[264] Kennedy ended with the suggestion that Mitchell had threatened to shoot a rival for Mrs. Annie Bowers's attentions, and the question was objected to and ruled out (presumably as improper character evidence). Still, the jurors had heard it.

Mitchell's testimony was followed by two lock experts who explained that the key found on Mitchell when he was arrested was a common type found in every locksmith's store and that the lock was of the cheapest variety and easily opened.[265]

Lynch then recalled John Weisman of Union City, with whom he had clashed earlier. Lynch asked Weisman what day the Jewish New Year was recorded on the Jewish calendar for 1909, and the witness said it had been on Friday, September 17.[266] Lynch asked Weisman if he was in Hartford on that day. The witness answered that he was in Hartford the night before but that he had returned to Union City on Friday morning and he then had gone back to Hartford on the noon train. Lynch then suggested that Weisman had told Michael Ashe and William Hard that he had never seen Mitchell at any time.[267] The witness denied this. It would seem that Lynch might have been onto something. Did the prosecution know about Weisman before Kennedy produced him? Did the state's lawyers think he was unreliable?[268] It is unethical to knowingly introduce perjured testimony. Is that why the prosecutors did not call Weisman in their case in chief? In any event, they took advantage of Weisman's testimony when it was offered by Kennedy, but they did not question him.[269]

Next up was Mrs. Annie Bowers, the "attractive blonde widow" Mitchell had been seeing. Her appearance drew some of the attention away from Sophie.[270] Annie was "stylishly dressed in a well-fitting suit of blue cloth and carried a costly set of furs. Her hat was one of the latest creations from the millinery parlors."[271] Mitchell had testified that he had been in her company on Friday, September 17, when he was alleged to be committing the crime.

Now she was called by Prosecutor Kellogg as a rebuttal witness. Mrs. Bowers testified that Joe Mitchell had come to her home on Friday night, September 17. She was surprised at the lateness of the visit, about twenty-five minutes to eleven that evening. He asked her for a glass and took a drink of what he said was bitters. He acted in a hurry and was out of breath. Mitchell had previously testified that he had met her on Bank Street and that she had asked him to bring her whiskey. When asked about this, Mrs. Bowers paused and then declared, "That is a falsehood." On cross she did admit that she had seen him that morning and that he had called on her that night. Kennedy pressed her on the question of whiskey, and she denied that he had ever brought her whiskey, and the "feathers on her hat acted as tho [sic] in a convulsion" as she shook her head.[272] Kennedy had scored yet another point.

Additional testimony was given by Deputy Coroner Makepeace that Sophie had never told him about any attempted assault by Ben. In response Kennedy attempted to elicit from Mary Clark, the matron at police headquarters, that Sophie had told her of such an attempted assault, but the judge would not permit it. Still, by means of his persistent questioning, Kennedy got across to the jury what he wanted them to hear, to the displeasure of the court.

A few other witnesses were called, among them Simon Hugo, a jailor at the New Haven jail, who identified a handkerchief taken from Sophie's cell. It bore a raised *R* and not a *K*, but the embroidery was similar to that on the handkerchief found at the crime scene. The court ruled it out.[273]

The closing arguments were about to begin.

Closing Arguments

It was March 24, 1910. The headline of the *Waterbury Republican* read "Brilliant Pleas Made for the Life of Kritchman Girl by Sen. Kennedy."[274] In other news of the world, the House of Representatives had just passed a bill providing money to raise the wreck of the battleship *USS Maine*. In Ohio a jailed Indiana banker had hit his turnkey on the head with an iron bar and broke jail. He had been on the run for three days and had worn out two posses and a couple of bloodhounds. He must have been almost as fast as the "Wizard of the Track," Barney Oldfield, who had just broken three world speed records.

Back at the Kritchman trial, it was decided that Prosecutor Kellogg would begin the closing arguments or summations, followed by Cassidy for Sophie, and then Michael Blansfield for Mitchell. After Blansfield, Kennedy would get a second chance for Sophie, followed by Lynch for Mitchell. The final argument for the state would be given by Prosecutor Alling. Judge Williams's charge would follow.[275]

Kellogg's summation was straightforward and logical. This was murder in the first degree, and the only issue for the jury was the identity of the perpetrators. He pointed to Ben's dying declarations.

> "I am shot to death…[by]…[a] Union City girl and a Waterbury fellow."…There was no need of an oath from that man lying with the fear of God in his heart to make it solemn. The evidence runs back time and time again to the same answer. There is no other answer.[276]

Kellogg was said to have been very dramatic as he told of Sophie's visit to the victim on Friday evening, accompanied by Victoria Dalton, when Sophie took the long, dark, shiny thing from her stocking and cut his throat. If Sophie's account had been truthful, why did she tell Victoria that if Victoria told her mother about what they had heard they would be arrested? As to Mitchell and his alibi, Kellogg reminded the jurors of the testimony of street conductor Monahan and of Mrs. Murphy. Curiously the newspaper accounts do not mention any discussion of Weisman, who had not testified in the first trial and had not been called by the prosecution—but instead had been produced by Kennedy. Did Kellogg have reason to doubt Weisman's truthfulness? Is that why Kellogg had not alluded to Weisman's story? Kellogg then went on to attack the expert testimony of Drs. Diefendorf and Johnson.

During his turn Cassidy pointed to Mitchell as the monster behind the crime. As he argued, Sophie poured out the tears.[277]

> Woman does not commit a crime in most cases unless behind it there is a man of low character. But how about a young woman, such as this girl is? Well educated and a teacher of little children, she was naturally of kind heart and could not have committed this crime…What motive could she have for murder?…Absolutely none, except to say that she wanted to marry Mitchell. But that cannot be so if you believe the testimony that she was engaged to Dr. Rutkauskas of Chicago and there can be no question about that. Then again it would be a physical impossibility for that girl to have done the shooting, for the testimony of Mr. Schneer, who sold her a revolver, was to the effect that she could not pull the trigger [of the revolver handed to her in the Superior Court in Waterbury] …Also remember the experiments of Mr. Bassett showing the distance at which powder will stain, and you will see how impossible it would be for this girl to shoot that man standing as close as she was to him and not stain his clothing.[278]

Kennedy argued that Victoria had changed her testimony from the first trial, and he also noted that there was no blood on Sophie's hands or clothing. Furthermore, if the "bloody note" had been written by Ben with the pencil found in the grass (but not produced at trial), why didn't it have a single puncture in it, he asked? Wouldn't there have been more blood on the note? It was a fake, he insisted.

On behalf of Mitchell, Blansfield summarized the queue of alibi witnesses and commented on the improbabilities of Sophie's testimony. He also noted the inconsistency between Mrs. Murphy's testimony that she saw Mitchell at eight o'clock Saturday morning and Sophie's claim that Mitchell came to Union City after nine o'clock that morning. He also ridiculed Sophie's story that Ben had attempted to assault her.[279]

Kennedy made the sort of melodramatic speech that the jurors of the day liked. It was reported that when he sat down there was hardly a dry eye. Of course, Kennedy claimed that he wanted a verdict guided by the evidence and not based on mercy for his client, which was totally disingenuous. "I pray that the verdict will be such that this little girl can say, 'Yes, mamma, I'll be home with you tonight.'"[280] He said these things as "tears flowed down his furrowed cheeks and his voice tremble[ed] with every syllable."[281] These were the days when it was said that if a lawyer could conjure up tears, he was obliged to do so.

Kennedy made much of his examination of Widow Bowers, arguing that Mitchell had lied about his visit to her, and he made much of Mitchell's conduct in bringing both the widow and Sophie to alcohol. Mitchell was trying to drag them down. The theme was belabored throughout the argument, for had he not said that there was a conspiracy against Sophie funded by rum? "You can't touch anything in this case, but that you find a liquor dealer in it. Even the man who brought Sophia to Waterbury in his automobile with the police, John J. Sheehan, is engaged in that business." Kennedy again stressed that the evidence showed that the bloodstained note had not been written by Ben but that it was a forgery. As for Sophie's purchase of a revolver, she had been "compelled to obey the dictates of a stronger mind." Any of Sophie's prior admissions had been wrung from her by the coroner's third-degree tactics.[282]

Lawyer Lynch spared Sophie nothing, nor would Prosecutor Alling. A reporter noted:

> As these remarks in which she was called a falsifier were directed at her she sat with a sneering smile on her face which at times almost broke into a laugh.[283]

Lynch went so far as to personally demonstrate how he could hold the revolver in his hand and pretend to pull the trigger as hard as he could, as the "muscles and tendons stood out on his arms," while he could have pulled the trigger easily had he wanted to. He ended his summation with the testimony of Ben, the one witness who could no longer speak. He read from the bloodstained note: "Sophie shot me, Sophia Kritchman, it seems I must die and at your hands at two after dinner."

Sophie just looked up and smiled.

Prosecutor Alling, who had worked under Judge Williams when the judge had been a prosecutor, argued that "Sophie had the courage, and Mitchell had the brains," but he was "yellow." He described the position that Sophie said she had been in when the victim was shot—on his left side, his arm around her neck. Mitchell could not have fired the shots "thru the bushes in the back of the two and hit [Ben] Kulvinskas in the stomach." Later, the impossibility of Sophie's version of the shooting—that the shots were fired by Mitchell—would be a point stressed by Mitchell's lawyers in their requested findings in aid of his appeal.

All in all, there had been pretty good lawyering on both sides. Now Judge Williams would give his instructions (or *charge*) to the jurors, and it would all then be in their hands.

Jury Instructions

Connecticut practice at the time called for the trial judge to give his charge to the jury after the closing arguments of counsel. That practice is common today, although in some jurisdictions the judge's charge precedes the closing arguments. That is so in the author's home state of Kentucky, a *frontier* state after the Revolution. The populations of such western states resented the power of British judges who had the last word on everything and who were permitted to deliver lengthy speeches to the jurors summing up the evidence and commenting on the testimony of the witnesses.[284] The power to comment is, if abused, the power to convict. In Kentucky the judge has no such power, and the instructions are expected to be rather bare bones, leaving the job of filling out things to the advocates. One would suspect that most trial lawyers like this frontier model. In Connecticut and in some other states and the federal courts, the judges have the power, at least in theory, to comment on the evidence.

Having the power to comment, Judge Williams exercised it, droning on. His charge to the jury takes up fifty-one single-spaced printed pages in Vol. 107 of *Connecticut Supreme Court Records and Briefs*, Third District, January Term (1911). The reading of the charge took nearly three hours.[285] It was reported that Judge Williams "dwelt much on the credibility of witnesses and had occasion frequently to refer to Sophie Kritchman's intimacy with Joe Mitchell, giving one the impression that the girl was not more than ordinarily mentally sound."[286] Among his more interesting pronouncements was one assessing the value of Ben's statement that he had been shot by a "Union City girl and a Waterbury fellow." Specifically Judge Williams stated that Ben and Sophie were friends, and "[i]t is therefore important for you to consider why [Ben]

Kulvinskas should make such an awful accusation against her [if it were not true, was the implication]."[287]

Again, there would be drama.

> Sophie's musical tendencies were brought to light in a new way to-day, when during the reading of the charge—the court room being silent as death—a band on the street struck up the notes of "My Country, 'Tis of Thee."

> Although she had listened to Judge Williams' review of the horrible evidence without the slightest sign of emotion, the music struck to her heart and before the first few bars had died away, the tears flowed down her cheeks in virtual streams.[288]

Among the judge's instructions to the jurors was the following:

> It is not claimed by or in behalf of either of the accused that [Ben] Kulvinskas was not killed by some person or persons or that there was any excuse or justification for such killing so far as they had any knowledge. Counsel for the accused, Sophia Kritchman, insist that Mitchell is guilty of the murder charged. Counsel for the accused, Mitchell, has strenuously maintained that Sophia Kritchman is guilty of the murder charged.

In other words, the judge viewed the case as one involving a cutthroat defense by both parties. Again, this was arguably not the case. Mitchell's defense was grounded in the proposition that he was not there and that he knew nothing about the victim's death. That is one reason why both defendants wanted separate trials. The judge also gave a charge on conspiracy—that there had been an agreement between Sophie and Mitchell beforehand to do the crime. Mitchell argued unsuccessfully the only evidence of that was the uncorroborated testimony of his codefendant about a plan hatched on Thursday, September 16. In his charge on conspiracy the judge pointed out to the jurors that each coconspirator was responsible for the acts of the other.

Another important point is that the judge gave the jurors the option of finding one or both defendants guilty of a lesser charge of second-degree murder or manslaughter. This invited a compromise verdict, which in the end, appears to have worked in Sophie's favor. Mitchell's appeal would raise both points but to no avail. Mitchell's counsel would also argue that the court erred by not including a standard cautionary charge given when an accomplice's evidence is offered to establish the guilt of an associate.

VERDICT AND SENTENCES

The jury was out only five or six hours.[289] When the jurors returned with a verdict of manslaughter for Sophie and second-degree murder for Mitchell, the story was covered in newspapers across the country.[290] Mitchell said nothing and did not move a muscle. Sophie had faced the jury with a smile, but now there was a moment of stunned silence. Then she sobbed as she was gathered up by Kennedy.[291]

At sentencing Kennedy made what was described as a "pathetic plea" for Sophie, claiming that she was showing signs of tuberculosis and that she could not be expected to live out a long sentence.[292] Judge Williams gave Mitchell life in prison, and he gave Sophie a sentence of twelve to fifteen years in the prison at Wethersfield.[293]

Wethersfield had been opened in 1827, and it must have been a grim and foreboding place. One of its most celebrated inmates was Amy Archer-Gilligan, the nursing home poisoner who inspired the play *Arsenic and Old Lace*. Archer-Gilligan was tried and found guilty in 1917. She was retried after a successful appeal in 1919 and convicted. One wonders whether she and Sophie ever met.

After the verdict against Sophie was announced, women in the audience crowded around Sophie and many made "obnoxious remarks." Kennedy had to get the deputies to form a flying wedge to get her out of the courtroom. Sophie still had a sense for the dramatic.

Oh, why was Judge Williams so cruel to me? He has not a particle of mercy in him. He did not give me a chance. He did not believe I was telling the truth, and I call upon God to witness that I was. The sentence will mean death to me and I wish he had sentenced me to be hung [sic] in the morning....

Cell block for women prisoners, Connecticut State Prison,
Wethersfield, Connecticut, circa 1910–1920 (25)

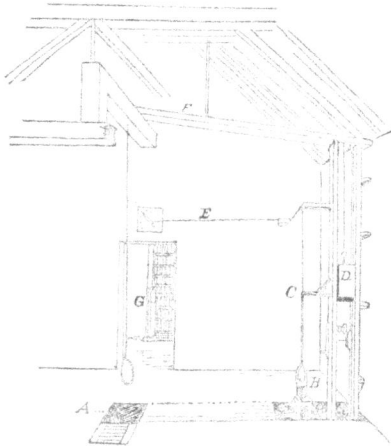

Jabez L. Woodbridge, warden of the Connecticut State Prison at Wethersfield
(1893–1899), patented this "automatic gallows," patent no. 541,409. Dr. Allan
McLane Hamilton credited Woodbridge with the "inventive genius of
New England…to make more merciful and successful the use of hanging…"
from Allan McLane Hamilton, *Recollections of an Alienist* 388 (1916). (26)

How this will please my enemies in Union City, those friends of Mitchell who conspired against me in this case. [The reporter noticed a "dangerous flash" in her eyes.] They did everything they could against me and now I hope they are satisfied that they have sent me to my death because I know I will not live more than a few months.²⁹⁴

Before her return to the jail, Sophie sent a telegram to Dr. Rutkauskas:

Dr. A. K. Rutkauskas, 8829 Commercial Avenue, Chicago, Ill. Loving one; I had my sentence just given to me; no less than Twelve years, no more than fifteen. Your Sophie.

Lawyer Lynch moved for a new trial for Joe Mitchell, arguing that it had been an error to order a joint trial. He attacked the witnesses who had broken Mitchell's alibi.

Mrs. Murphy...said she saw him [Mitchell] in her back yard at 8 o'clock in the morning on Friday, Sept. 17, and we know he could not have been there at that hour. Mrs. Murphy said she saw him wearing a light suit of clothes, as light as that worn by Deputy Coroner Makepeace. Has the state been able to substantiate that claim?

Then there is Monahan, the streetcar conductor. Monahan said he saw him on his car some time on Friday and Saturday. Then he said "you see Frank Nolan and he'll tell you what day he was on that car." You heard Nolan say that he was not on the back platform of the car at any time. There is John Weisman. We know that Weisman's son went with the state policeman to see witnesses and when Weisman told his story he was not put on by the state. His word was not considered reliable. We proved that he was in Hartford on the Thursday night preceding the tragedy and that he was there on Friday. He tells you that he came home on Friday morning and went back on the noon train. It was at the same hour that Mrs. Bowers placed him [Mitchell] in Waterbury.²⁹⁵

Amy Archer-Gilligan, the nursing home poisoner who inspired *Arsenic and Old Lace* written by American playwright Joseph Kesselring (27)

Mitchell's lawyer also injected a new argument that Sophie's uncorroborated testimony was incompetent because she was suffering from delusions associated with paresis. Was he talking about general paresis of the insane (GPI)—inflammation of the brain caused by syphilis? At one time the mental condition of paresis was thought to be caused by everything from overwork to excess in drink or sex, a madness due to dissolute character, and was more common in men than women.[296] But the link between general paresis and syphilis[297] appears to have been pretty well established by the time of the Kritchman trials. Perhaps not, at least not in the mind of the lawyer. It should also be pointed out that GPI is associated with tertiary syphilis, with symptoms appearing long after infection (ten to thirty years). One would think that Sophie would have been much too young to have suffered from it.

Mitchell's lawyer's claim must have been startling. Had any evidence been presented at trial to prove this? No discussion of it was found in the newspapers. Moreover, if the question was of her competency as a witness, one would think that this would have been taken up with the court before Sophie testified.

The whole thing seems like little more than grasping at straws—a last minute Hail Mary.

Note also that the jury probably (perhaps not necessarily) found Weisman to be credible, and the credibility of witnesses is a question for the jury. (Later, in a parole hearing, it would be charged that he had committed perjury, but there was never any finding to that effect and no action was ever taken against him.) The motion for a new trial was denied.[298]

The verdict came as a surprise to many observers. The savagery of the killing fully justified a conviction of one or the other defendants for first-degree murder, and most agreed that the manslaughter verdict for Sophie was a big legal victory for Kennedy and Cassidy.[299] Reporters noted that the trial "was the longest ever held in this state, and it was also the most expensive, costing the state many thousands of dollars."[300] A news article dated May 24, 1910, reported that the bills totaled around $20,000.[301]

PART FOUR

Springtime for Sophie

THE APPEAL

The appellate records of the case can be found in Vol. 107 of *Connecticut Supreme Court Records and Briefs*, Third District, January Term (1911). Although the case is titled *State of Connecticut v. Joseph Pecciulis, alias Joseph Mitchell, and Sophie Kritchman*, only Mitchell participated as an appellant. In the state reports, the opinion of the court is styled *State v. Pecciulis (Joseph).*[302] Mitchell's appellate counsel was the firm of Stoddard, Goodhart & Stoddard. I am speculating, but I assume that Sophie's counsel advised that she had gotten the best she could have expected, despite all the weeping and gnashing of teeth. Although her lawyers filed a notice of appeal, it does not look like they went any further.[303]

Connecticut procedure at the time called for the trial judge to draft findings in aid of the appeal. That meant that the parties had to offer objections and proposed additions to the findings, which the judge was not bound to accept. Mitchell's counsel offered a number of revisions to add to or rectify the judge's proposed findings. All were rejected.

As to errors in rulings on points of evidence at trial, Mitchell's brief complained, *inter alia* (I am paraphrasing and commenting on the arguments):

1. That the trial judge had improperly limited the cross-examination of Patrick Monahan, the trolley car conductor through whom an attempt was made to place Mitchell in Union City on Saturday, September 18, and to prove that Sophie was on the same car. Lynch wanted to impeach Monahan with his inconsistent grand jury testimony. The judge's ruling seems inexplicable.

2. That the trial judge improperly limited the cross-examination
    of lawyer McGrath as to what had transpired at the hospital,
    particularly regarding Mitchell's reaction of surprise when
    [Ben] Kulvinskas accused him. Prosecutors often argue that
    the suspect's conduct after the event tends to prove conscious-
    ness of guilt. Lynch was suggesting, to use trial lawyer lingo,
    that "what's sauce for the goose is sauce for the gander." That
    is, that his reactions exhibited consciousness of innocence.

3. Likewise, that the trial judge did not permit Dr. Pomeroy to
    testify as to Mitchell's reaction of surprise, upon Prosecutor
    Kellogg's objection that the question called for a conclusion.
    Lynch argued that the witness was reciting his personal
    observations, which suggested the accused's consciousness
    of innocence. The court observed that the testimony would
    have been *self-serving.*

4. That the trial judge should not have admitted Sophie's
    answer on cross-examination to the question: What did
    he [Ben Kulvinskas] say by volunteering, "When we got
    there somebody hollered out of the bushes, 'Shut up, or
    I'll kill you.' We got afraid and we run back. I thought it
    was Mitchell that was up in the bushes there." Lynch
    apparently moved to strike the answer as nonrespon-
    sive to the question put to her and injected speculation.

Mitchell's brief also stressed the fact that Ben said he had never
seen Mitchell at any point when he received his multiple wounds and
that the charge of the court never directed the jury's attention to this.
Mitchell's complaints about the charge also challenged the sufficiency of
the evidence said to support the charge of conspiracy used by the judge
to justify a joint trial.

Mitchell's lawyers again raised the argument that Sophie's testimony
was not competent evidence because she was suffering at the time from
paresis and that this was "shown by her various love affairs and the way

in which she discussed them."[304] Again, nothing was found about paresis in the newspaper accounts of the trial other than the allusion to it in Mitchell's motion for a new trial, and assuming that there was anything to the contention, evidence regarding this medical condition would have had to have been introduced at trial to preserve the issue for appeal. A brief newspaper account of the appeal states that the argument was based on "the assumption that she was suffering from paranoia."[305]

This account accurately reflects the argument in the brief on behalf of Mitchell (Joseph Pecciulis) that Sophie's testimony was deluded—or the product of delusions—and "would indicate, according to every medical authority on this subject, that this woman was suffering from an insane delusion known as paranoia."[306] The brief cited no medical testimony in the record to support this, so it seems fair to characterize this as a lawyers' argument about the plausibility or credibility of Sophie's testimony. The jurors were invited to draw the inference that Sophie was deluded and that her testimony should not be given any weight, but they apparently did not do so. Moreover, general paresis of the insane, which appears in the late stages of syphilis, seems unlikely given Sophie's subsequent history.

As to the claimed errors in evidentiary rulings, the appellate court held that the trial judge had not abused his discretion in making any of his rulings. And, as to the omission of a cautionary instruction regarding the uncorroborated testimony of an accomplice, the court pointed to the dying declaration as corroborating evidence and made the following observation, which the reader may want to take with a grain of salt:

> There is nothing in the record before us that justifies the inference that the state offered Sophia Kritchman as a witness to prove the guilt of Mitchell. On the contrary, it is fair to assume from the finding that her testimony was given when she was speaking as a witness in her own defense.

All other complaints regarding the instructions were turned aside by the Supreme Court of Errors.

INCARCERATION

Sophie Kritchman and Joe Mitchell went off to prison,[307] but that is not the end of the story. Sophie was still newsworthy. On April 5, 1910, the following story appeared:

SOPHIE KRITCHMAN GOES TO PRISON LAUGHING

Sophie Kritchman…passed through Hartford on her way to the state prison at Wethersfield and acted as if her journey's end were a lovers' meeting instead of a long confinement within a prison's walls. She laughed and talked, found pleasure in thinking that she was recognized on the street, pointed out places on the way which were a remembered part of her environment while she lived in this city, and in general seemed to feel very happy and satisfied.… The merry strains of a street piano made her want to dance. She saw some music in the window of one of the music stores that she passed…and wanted to go in and buy a song, 'The Visions of Love.' A week ago she was raving in jail and had to be drugged with morphine to keep her quiet.[308]

Sophie had not been long at Wethersfield when, shortly after Mitchell's appeal was denied, she began to behave in such a way that the acting warden asked Governor Simeon Baldwin to transfer her to the Connecticut General Hospital for the Insane at Middletown.[309] Dr. Diefendorf, *who had been one of the defense expert witnesses*, was associated with this asylum. Coincidently, as previously mentioned, Amy Archer-Gilligan, the poisoner, would also move in there in 1924.

Sophie could not have been too crazy. She functioned well enough to win the *tennis championship* at the asylum.[310] In those days it was thought that athletic competition was a good treatment for those with mental issues. The Middletown State Homeopathic Hospital in New York (not Connecticut) had a baseball team called the "Asylums" that for a time dominated semipro play in the Lower Hudson Valley. In 1891 they almost beat the New York Giants of the National League.[311]

Sophie also wrote verse[312] and copyrighted songs ironically titled "My Last Good-Bye"[313] and "I Live For Thee."[314]

It was suggested that Sophie was "quite the little actress,"[315] and she went so far as to order a piano from a Waterbury music dealer, who was "hot under the collar" when he went to Middletown only to learn that his would-be purchaser was in the state hospital.[316] A September 10, 1913, newspaper story reported that she had become violent and sawed the bars of her cell window, but the story did not pan out.[317]

In the end, Sophie was returned to prison after being pronounced sane by physicians.[318] Ten years into her sentence she was hoping to be released by the parole board, but she would be disappointed.[319]

Meanwhile, Joe Mitchell was not taking things lying down. A new lawyer, Jesse Devine, entered an appearance with affidavits which supposedly proved that, as Lynch had argued, Mitchell had been the victim of perjury. Devine assisted Mitchell in applying for a pardon,[320] but such things take time. Mitchell was still in prison in 1918, when he and a number of other prisoners volunteered to serve in the war in France.[321]

Sophie's Release and Return
to Waterbury

In July 1919, Sophie was looking forward to going home after eleven years in prison.[322] She was released May 8, 1920, and returned to Waterbury, accompanied by her mother and her lawyer.[323] By September 1920, it was reported that she was to marry a Lithuanian named Alfonz Sakatanskas of Naugatuck, who had come to this country while she was in prison.[324] The prospective groom's name was spelled a number of ways—for example, as Alfred Sokoloski in a story titled "Springtime for Sophie Kritchman."[325]

I am reminded of the famous trial of Maria Barbella, who escaped death in the electric chair in 1896. She had slit the throat of Domenico Cataldo and was convicted and sentenced to die; but she was acquitted in a second trial, the jury buying the argument that she had done the deed while in a fit of "psychic epilepsy."[326] Dr. Allan McLane Hamilton, the famous neurologist and grandson of Alexander Hamilton, who had been involved in the background of the case for the prosecution, noted that "Maria subsequently married a man who must have been quite devoid of the emotion of fear."[327]

It was reported that Sophie received offers from "moving pictures concerns" and requests from newspapers to do a story of her life. Surprisingly she turned them down. She had finally had enough of the limelight.[328]

Mitchell and the Board of Pardons

Mitchell's appeal to the Board of Pardons was noted in the press in June 1922.[329] A wealthy Waterbury real estate man named Louis M. Raffel was rallying support. Affidavits collected by Raffel attacked Weisman in particular, and Mrs. Mary Murphy provided an affidavit saying that she was not allowed to tell her story "in her own way." She now said that she had not been sure that it was Mitchell whom she had seen. Six of the jurors who convicted Mitchell said that they might have reached a different verdict if they had had this information.[330]

Affidavits were also provided from former Police Chief Schmidt and Deputy Coroner Makepeace, who were now of the view that if Mitchell had been involved at all, it was as an accomplice.[331] A hearing was set on the petition.[332] On Tuesday morning, December 18, 1923, the following headline appeared in *The Bridgeport Telegram*:

JOE MITCHELL AND 7 OTHERS FREED BY PARDON BOARD—
Claim of 'Twisted Testimony' Helps Liberate One of Principals in
Notorious Kritchman Case[333]

The next day Raffel announced that there were definite plans for Mitchell's future and that a fund had been established to help him. There was a plan to buy him a farm. A special passport would be arranged to bring his aged mother to America.[334] The same newspaper article noted that Sophie Kritchman had called upon Governor Charles Templeton and asked him to use his influence to block Mitchell's release. The governor told her he would be guided by the evidence in the case.[335]

Not everyone was satisfied. There were calls for the removal of the state's attorney at New Haven—an office filled by Arnold A. Alling—for "railroading" Mitchell. There were also demands that John Weisman be removed from his position as deputy sheriff of Waterbury.[336] A mass meeting was scheduled, and the governor was invited. Two local priests, Father Murray and Father Fanning, were active in these resolutions, which alarmed church authorities. It was suggested that these priests were acting in an unethical manner by participating in such goings-on. The higher ecclesiastical authorities were less concerned with the fact that a mistake may have been made than they were that respect for law and order and its institutions might be eroded by any suggestion that court officials might have done something wrong.[337] Soon the state's judges began to wake up, concerned that the proles were getting stirred up and that "ignorant people were being led to believe that the system of jurisprudence in Connecticut permitted the unscrupulous to throw innocent foreigners into state prison for life."[338] There was fear that any proclamation of Mitchell's innocence would be most unfortunate.

Governor Templeton was made aware of the controversy. Indeed, it was reported that lawyer Lynch warned him not to appear at any public gathering. Presumably Lynch was pragmatic—he wanted Mitchell released, and trouble might make the whole thing that much more difficult. The governor was persuaded not to attend the mass meeting. He presided over the hearing of the Board of Pardons. Mitchell was freed, but no formal grounds for his pardon were stated.[339] There was no finding that Weisman perjured himself, and there was no determination that Mitchell was innocent.

All the publicity surrounding the pardon proceedings more or less drowned out another side of the story. It seems that Raffel had instigated a petition calling for Weisman's removal from office as early as December 1922, and the petition included charges that Weisman "had been using his influence as an officer of the Kingsbury Street synagogue—Beth Israel—to adjust official business."[340] That is to say, there was a personal feud between the two. Weisman sued Raffel for defamation in late July 1923 on account of Raffel's accusations that Weisman[341] had committed perjury in the Kritchman-Mitchell trial. The lawsuit was mentioned in the press under a headline "Waterbury Greets 'Joe' Mitchell."[342] Another story suggested that Mitchell had somehow been "used" in the feud between Raffel and Weisman, who were described as "both rich and prominent in Hebrew activities of Waterbury."[343] In an interview with representatives of the *Hartford Courant* (Raffel declined an interview), Weisman argued that Raffel had developed an interest in Mitchell only after their feud heated up, suggesting that the charge of false testimony was simply another personal attack by Raffel.[344]

Weisman won the libel suit and was awarded $3,000 in damages. He had sought $50,00, but the wise litigant asks for the kitchen sink—and $3,000 in 1924 would be worth almost $43,000 today.[345]

Afterword

The preface promised a bit more about William Thomas Walsh's novel *Out of the Whirlwind*. The reader will recall that Walsh said, in an author's note, that he "made no effort to relate, save in the barest outline, the story of the actual crime" that had inspired his novel. (We are reminded of the fictitious persons disclaimer that appears in works, putting the reader on notice that all characters appearing in the story are fictitious and that all resemblances to real persons, living or dead, are purely coincidental.) Still, the first 273 pages of 479 pages of the novel closely track the investigation and trials in the *Kritchman* case. A reader of the time could easily identify Hookerstown as Waterbury. The local paper is the *Hookerstown Herald* instead of the *Waterbury Republican*. Sophia Kritchman appears as Nina Mateskas, a young music teacher who views herself as the "heroine of a continuous play." Ben Kulvinskas becomes Casimir Pavlonis. A character like Antone, Ben Kulvinskas's brother, appears as a friend named Stanislaus. Joe Mitchell becomes Steven West. Kennedy becomes the insidious and highly successful lawyer Francis P. Scanlon. Prosecutor Kellogg appears as Allen B. Ackley, who is described as "the meanest prosecutor in New England." Mitchell's trial lawyer is the amiable and honest Ignatius Kelly, who is later killed in the Great War.

Walsh has Nina get the gun from Casimir's trunk. She has two guns now—the gun from the trunk and the gun she purchased. The victim of the crime is found in a similar condition, with virtually identical wounds, in a spot similar to that in the real murder. Even the "bloody note" found at the scene is like the one found in the *Kritchman* case.

What is slightly different is that Casimir and his note were found by Constable Jake Greenhut, who will turn out to be the principal villain

in the story. Greenhut is the creature of—and the debtor of—lawyer
Scanlon. Indeed, Greenhut's son has gone into practice with Scanlon
after his graduation from law school, just before the first Mateskas
trial. Lawyer Scanlon takes on Sophie's defense. He gets to Greenhut
before Greenhut can tell anyone else all he knows (or suspects he knows).
Greenhut has a note coming due, and he asks Scanlon to endorse it.
Scanlon gets Greenhut talking about the Mateskas business.

Greenhut's theory, which he spells out to Scanlon, was that Nina was
a "warm baby" who was going around with a number of men. West was
serious about Nina and wanted to marry her. Nina had rejected Casimir,
and Casimir threatened to tell West about Nina's other men. So, Nina
"bump[ed] Casimir off." Greenhut tells Scanlon that he saw Nina on
Friday, coming from the murder scene and walking alone, and he also
saw her walking along the same road Saturday morning, again alone.
He only saw West later Saturday when Nina got West to go to the scene
of the crime with her. In Walsh's version of the crime, Nina finishes off
Casimir in the presence of a surprised and horrified West.

Of course, this is not what Scanlon wanted to hear. After satisfying
himself that Greenhut has not told what he knows or suspects to anyone
else, Scanlon explains that Greenhut's version would hurt the case of his
client, Nina. He tells Greenhut that he is glad that Greenhut hasn't told
his story to anyone else. He craftily assures Greenhut that he wouldn't
want Greenhut to perjure himself or to hold back the truth in anyway,
and he adds, "You understand me?"[346] Needless to say, Greenhut does
understand, at least what Scanlon wants.

Scanlon then gives Greenhut a preview of the closing argument
that he plans to give to the jury. He spins the story to Greenhut and
an imaginary jury that West compelled Nina—what could this "poor
defenseless little girl" have done? Even if she went to the scene alone, she
may have done so out of pity, to help Casimir after West told her of his
crime, and then she may have run away frightened.

Then he turns to Greenhut and tells him that he thinks Greenhut is
wrong about seeing her alone on Saturday morning. Greenhut gets it.
Yes, he was mistaken about that, says Greenhut. "I thought so. Good!"
responds Scanlon, confident that his instructions have been understood.

Greenhut lies at trial by "positively" identifying West as having been at the scene of the crime early on Friday and Saturday. So the villains of Walsh's novel are the girl's defense lawyer and his perjured lackey. The lawyer is able to shift the blame to Nina's innocent codefendant, but this blame-shifting is not entirely a lawyer-generated theory, as it may be in many real cases. In the novel it had already been Nina's plan, which she had disclosed to West in a threat when he said he would turn her in.

There are two trials, the first ending in a mistrial after a note threatening Nina is sent to the court. One difference from the real story is that in the book both trials are of the two defendants jointly. The judge is Judge Harris in the role of Judges Curtis and Williams.

Nina blames everything on West. West presents his alibi witnesses, but Greenhut blows a hole in the alibi. Nina gets twelve to fifteen years for manslaughter. West is sentenced to death, but the execution is not carried out. Judge Harris goes on to become governor, and Scanlon goes to Washington as a congressman (as did the real lawyer Kennedy, by the way).

As I noted previously, there was never any determination that Weisman committed perjury. He was never formally charged with anything. He must have gotten some feeling of vindication when he won his libel case. Furthermore, as far as I can tell, nobody ever charged Kennedy with any wrongdoing. There was no suggestion that he urged a witness to lie or that he *knew* a witness was lying. Kennedy's duty was to defend Sophie zealously, within the bounds of law. A lawyer who presents testimony *knowing* that a witness is committing perjury may be disciplined for professional misconduct and in an appropriate case may be charged with subornation of perjury. If the witness is not the criminal defendant but rather a non-party witness, the defense lawyer has professional discretion to choose not to present the testimony if the lawyer reasonably believes the witness is lying (but does not *know* the witness is lying), but the lawyer is not *required* to withhold the testimony.[347] There is some wiggle room here. There must be. Walsh's Scanlon looks like a bad actor. Novelist Walsh can put thoughts in his head and words in his mouth. I do not feel free to do that.

Most of the remainder of *Out of the Whirlwind* is devoted to West's Job-like struggle and redemption. He is not hanged, and after ten years in prison he is freed through the efforts of a millionaire named Henry Kaplan,[348] who stands in for the real-life Raffel and who proves Greenhut's perjury. Greenhut commits suicide.[349] This suicide is an odd twist in Walsh's story, especially ironic, because in the beginning of the novel Greenhut's father is found dead—murdered or a suicide. Midwife Juggie Duhan told Nina that it was probably murder, but the coroner ruled it a suicide, and no one ever paid for the crime. This inspired Nina to try something similar, but she botched the job. The word *overkill* comes to mind.

It has been said that "[l]awyers in criminal cases, for prosecution and defense, sometimes swim in a sea of lies."[350] Sometimes the lies are client lies, sometimes an opponent's lies, and sometimes, it is sad to say, a lawyer's lies. Such things happen.

One may also speculate as to Joe Mitchell's guilt. Many of the witnesses on both sides of the case seem a bit shaky and partisan. Was this a case in which a "guilty man was framed" (a popular trope in fiction—and sometimes fact)? Who can say for sure? In any event, governors exercise their own judgment in the pardon process and are not bound by the rules that limit the power of appellate courts.

I tried to track down what happened to Joe Mitchell after his release from prison, to see how things worked out for him. Quite by chance, I found a scrapbook in the records of the Connecticut Historical Society (Volume 47, June 1920) that contained several clippings relating to the case. One reports that Joe Mitchell wed Miss Browny Kachergis in 1924.[351] Sadly, I found this account in *The Day* (New London, Connecticut), dated April 8, 1925:

JOE MITCHELL, PARDONED FOR MURDER DIES –
Man Who Served 14 Years Maintains Innocence to Last

Waterbury, April 8 – Joe Mitchell, recently pardoned from the state prison at Wethersfield after serving 14 years of life sentence for the alleged murder of Ben Kulvinskas in Naugatuck was buried today. The funeral was largely attended and an extra automobile was needed to carry the flowers. Mitchell died of heart disease.

In a little dingy room in the tenement at 311 Washington Avenue, where he made his home with his bride of less than a year, Joe Mitchell Monday night passed out of life, which to him had been a real tragedy. A heart weakened by the rigor of prison work and confinement which could not stand the acceleration of joy caused by his release and the happiness his wedding brought him caused his death.

Mitchell dies maintaining his innocence of the crime, forgiving those on whose testimony he had been convicted, and thanking all those who had come to his rescue at practically the close of his life to help vindicate him and spare him the disgrace of dying in state prison…

After the trials of Sophie Kritchman were over, Antone Kulvinskas sold the saloon at the corner of Anderson and School streets in Union City and left town. Since the opening of the saloon, bad luck [had] attended the brothers. Reverses met with during the early part of their venture lost them the benefit of profits from the business for many months, and just as the brothers had reached a successful foundation for their business, one met death and left the other to conduct the business which Antone [now] styled "a hoodoo."[352]

Lawyer William Kennedy, a former state senator and then, later, a congressman, became a force in the Democratic Party and an advisor to President Woodrow Wilson. But Kennedy died in 1918, before Mitchell's release from prison.[353] John Weisman died at his home in Waterbury on October 4, 1927, the day after being elected constable by the people of Waterbury, some years before Walsh published his novel.[354]

Acknowledgments

I am indebted to Michael C. Dooling, archivist at the Mattatuck Museum in Waterbury and former news librarian at the *Republican-American,* for his comments and assistance. He briefed me on the geography of Naugatuck and provided lots of tidbits regarding people and places appearing in the story. I must also thank Mel Smith and Debra Pond of the Connecticut State Library, who were able to provide me with newspapers and the surviving official documentation of the case.

Unfortunately, I was not able to find a full transcript of the trial testimony, but fragments were available in the trial and appellate records, and the excellent newspaper reporting was almost like daily transcripts from a court reporter—what we lawyers call *daily record*. The newspapers and other source material are listed in the selected bibliography.

Having said that this is not a work of fiction, I must also add that it is not necessarily the truth. I could only try to assemble and structure what was reported by others over one hundred years ago. Furthermore, the record is far from complete. Francis Bacon said, "Truth is the daughter, not of authority, but of time."[355] But time, too, can take its toll.

NOTES

Preface

1. Richard H. Underwood, *Mr. Howe's Last Case*, XXXI Legal Stud. F. 801 (2007).

2. RICHARD H. UNDERWOOD, GASLIGHT LAWYERS: CRIMINAL TRIALS & EXPLOITS IN GILDED AGE NEW YORK (2017).

3. RICHARD H. UNDERWOOD, CRIMESONG: TRUE CRIME STORIES FROM SOUTHERN MURDER BALLADS (2016).

4. Mara Bovsun, *He Named His Killers*, N.Y. DAILY NEWS, May 17, 2009. See also *From The International Herald Tribune, 100, 75, 50 Years Ago*, N.Y. TIMES, Feb. 4, 2010.

5. 84 Conn. 152, 79 A. 75 (1911), sometimes cited as *State v. Kritchman et al.* or *State v. Pecciulis (Joseph)*.

6. *See* Michael Dooling, *1909 Murder Made for Courtroom Drama*, THE REPUBLICAN AMERICAN, July 27, 2009.

7. WM. J. PAPE, I HISTORY OF WATERBURY AND THE NAUGATUCK VALLEY 17 (1918).

8. *See Notre Dame Honors Ex-Local Teacher*, THE HARTFORD COURANT, Mar. 24, 1941.

9. *Readable Novel with a Purpose*, COURIER JOURNAL, July 28, 1935. ("From old newspaper files Mr. Walsh took the none-too-pleasant details of a murder trial which took place in a factory town of Connecticut early in this century.") A reviewer in the *Tampa Times* breathlessly reported that "one feels they [the characters in the book] actually did some of the almost unbelievable things detailed. Especially this is true of the Arch-murderess who butchered her suitor in a wooded rendezvous and then charged the murder to her lover." Tampa Times, Tampa, FL, May 24, 1935. (Well, "they" actually did—and "she" actually did—these things.)

10. *Story of Crime in Connecticut*, The Hartford Courant, Sept. 8, 1935.

11. *Injection of Religion Occasionally Mars the Narration*, Tampa Times, *supra* note 9.

12. "*Out of the Whirlwind* is a bit too long for this reviewer and he is not an impatient man." *Id.*

13. *Kirkus Reviews*, May 6, 1935.

14. *Id.*

15. The Brooklyn Citizen, June 14, 1935.

16. For an interesting discussion of dying declarations in law and literature, see Peter Brooks, "Dying Declarations," Chapter 3.1 in Fictional Discourse and the Law, ed. Hans J. Lind (2020).

17. Nowadays the exception may apply even if the declarant lived, but the exception cannot be evoked unless the declarant is otherwise unavailable for trial for some other reason. *See, e.g.*, Federal Rule of Evidence 804(b)(2).

18. *See, e.g., Die Another Day: Ohio Court Finds Victim's Clicking Noises Qualify as Dying Declarations*, EvidenceProfBlog, (Colin Miller, ed.) Oct. 17, 2014, http://lawprofessors.typepad.com/evidenceprof/2014/10/according-to-an-article-in-theledger-enquirer-three-years-ago-calvin-grimes-lay-in-intensive-care-paralyzed-from-the-nec.html (last visited June 6, 2025); *Blink, Take 2: Ohio Court of Appeals Deems Blinking Evidence Admissible as a Dying Declaration*, EvidenceProfBlog, (Colin Miller, ed.) Sept. 12, 2014, http://lawprofessors.typepad.com/evidenceprof/2014/09/back-in-july-i-posedan-entryabout-state-v-hailes2014-wl-2191405-mdapp-2014-in-which-the-court-of-special-appeals-of-m.html (last visited June 6, 2025). In an even more recent case: The jury listened to a 911 call, during which the victim was asked who shot him, and he answered what sounded like, "Why man," and also said, "Deshaw Hacker, Deshay D., and William Rice," and "Deshawn Hacker." The defendant [appellant in the appeal from his conviction] Deshay Hacker went by the name "Wireman." A police officer at the scene, Brewer, testified at trial that he had asked the dying victim, "Was it Deshay?" and that the victim nodded his head yes. However, the officer was wearing a body camera and the head nod was not captured on the camera. The trial court admitted the head nod testimony as a dying declaration. On appeal, the defendant contended that the head nod, which was not captured by the camera, was too ambiguous to be

considered a nonverbal dying declaration, given the victim's suffering and agonal movements. The appellate court ruled that the trial judge did not abuse his discretion in admitting the evidence. The defendant/appellant's arguments went to the weight, and not the admissibility, of the evidence. The appellate opinion is *Hacker v. Indiana*, Court of Appeals Case 19A-CR-1577 (Ind. Ct. App., Jan. 12, 2021).

19. *See Giles v. California*, 554 U.S. 353 (2008); *Michigan v. Bryant*, 562 U.S. 344 (2011).

20. *See* Brandon L. Garrett, Convicting the Innocent: Where Criminal Prosecutions Go Wrong (2011).

21. The Maria Barbella trial in 1896 and the trial of Nan Patterson in 1905 come to mind. *See* Richard H. Underwood, Gaslight Lawyers (2017).

22. Lawrence B. Goodheart, Female Capital Punishment: From the Gallows to Unofficial Abolition in Connecticut 129-130 (2020).

23. *Id.* at 144.

24. Goodheart at 129, quoting *Sophie Beams As Juror Is Examined*, The Hartford Courant, Jan. 27, 1910.

Waterbury ("Brass City") and Naugatuck

25. Edith Reynolds and John Murray, Wicked Waterbury: Madmen & Mayhem in the Brass City (Kindle) (2008).

26. A good post on the history of Waterbury and birth control can be found at Raechel Guest's Waterbury Thoughts Blog, http://waterburythoughts. blogspot.com/2012/02/birth-control-some-history.html (last visited June 6, 2025).

27. Michael M. Greenburg, The Mad Bomber of New York: The Extraordinary True Story of the Manhunt That Paralyzed a City (2011).

28. *See* Michael Cannell, *Unmasking the Mad Bomber*, Smithsonian Magazine, Apr. 2017. https://www.smithsonianmag.com/history/ unmasking-the-mad-bomber-180962469/ (last visited June 6, 2025).

29. Reynolds and Murray, *supra* note 25 (not paginated).

30.   SUNDAY REPUBLICAN (Waterbury, CT), Jan. 30, 1910.

Sophie and Friends

31.   *How Old Is Miss Sophia Kritchman*, NAUGATUCK DAILY NEWS, Jan. 31, 1910; *Defense Begun in Kritchman Trial*, NAUGATUCK DAILY NEWS, Feb. 3, 1910; *Murder Trial—Birth Certificate Presented in Court Today Shows Pretty Music Teacher is 24 Years Old*, Bridgeport Evening Farmer, Feb. 3, 1910.

32.   All of these assessments of Sophie can be found at *Twelve Bullets Found in Cullwinshky's Body*, NAUGATUCK DAILY NEWS, SEPT. 20, 1909.

33.   *Sophia Kritchman's Pleas in Murder Case Will Be 'Not Guilty'*, WATERBURY REPUBLICAN, JAN. 23, 1910; *TRYING WOMAN FOR MURDER*, THE HARTFORD COURANT, Jan. 26, 1910; *Love Letters of Girl Are Read to Jurymen in Kritchman Trial*, WATERBURY REPUBLICAN, Mar. 12, 1910.

34.   *Sophia Kritchman Scores As Witness Against an Expert*, WATERBURY REPUBLICAN, Jan. 28, 1910.

35.   *Id.*

36.   *Kritchman Verdict: Sophia Guilty*, WATERBURY REPUBLICAN, Mar. 26, 1910 (containing a post-verdict history of the case).

37.   *Sophia Kritchman's Pleas in Murder Case Will Be 'Not Guilty,'* WATERBURY REPUBLICAN, Jan. 23, 1910.

38.   Judge Williams's Findings, Nos. 8 and 27, July 19, 1910.

39.   Judge Williams's Findings, No. 9, July 19, 1910.

Part One: As Ben Lay Dying

The Scene of the Crime

40.   *Brutal Murder at Union City*, WATERBURY REPUBLICAN, Sept. 19, 1909.

41.   Judge Williams's Findings, No. 24, July 19, 1910; *see also Dying Declarations; Blood Stained Note*, NAUGATUCK DAILY NEWS, Mar. 4, 1910.

42. *Twelve Bullet Wounds Found in Cullwinski's Body*, Naugatuck Daily News, Sept. 20, 1909.

43. *See Jealousy of Rival Motive Which Leads to Atrocious Crime*, Waterbury Republican, Sept. 20, 1909.

44. I am relying here on the Findings of Fact made by the trial judge in aid of the appeal in the case, dated July 19, 1910. Here is the relevant finding, dated July 19, 1910:

> 1. That about noon on the 13th of September, 1909, Bronislow Kulvinskas (called Ben) was found lying upon the ground in a secluded spot in the town of Waterbury near the boundary line between the towns of Waterbury and Naugatuck and near a wire fence on the northerly side of a grass covered and very infrequently used old road (called the New England road) and between the fence and bushes which were growing upon the northerly side of said road. This road was formerly the westerly part of a public highway leading from Union City in the town of Naugatuck to the passenger station (long since removed) upon what was formerly the New York and New England Railroad (now the Highland Division) of the New York, New Haven, and Hartford Railroad Company).
>
> Michael Dooling, whom I mention in the acknowledgments, believes that another way of locating "the Nook" would be just off Spring Street (now Route 68) to the Town Plot section of Waterbury (Highland Avenue). He does not believe that the "New England road" was ever really a street or a pedestrian road as such.

45. Judge Williams's Findings, No. 24, July 19, 1910; *Court Admits More Dying Declarations*, Naugatuck Daily News, Mar. 7, 1910; *State Rests in Kritchman Murder Case*, Waterbury Republican, Mar. 8, 1910.

46. *Id.* Who said what to whom is confusing. The finding from which much of this is drawn was a composite of different witnesses' testimonies.

47. *Murder Trial of Sophie and Joe Mitchell on Today*, Bridgeport Evening Farmer, Mar. 7, 1910. *State Rests Its Case in Kritchman Trial*, The Hartford Courant, Mar. 7, 1910.

48. Consider the 1930s "Head and Hands Murder," involving the killing of Cincinnati Fire Captain Harry Miller. His head and hands had been cut off, encased in concrete, and thrown into a lake in Carrollton, Kentucky.

The torso was hidden under a culvert and covered with rocks. When the body minus head and hands was found, the coroner held an on-the-spot inquest and returned a verdict of suicide. *See* WILLIAM FOSTER HOPKINS, MURDER IS MY BUSINESS 99 (1970). Perhaps even stranger was the case of Mrs. Addie Sheatsley, wife of Columbus, Ohio, minister Clarence Sheatsley, whose body was found in the furnace, burned up all the way to the waist. Her body would have been a tight fit, and the door was closed behind her. Her back was toward the opening. An expert hired by the prosecutor reported that there was no trace of carbon monoxide, soot, or ashes in her lungs, which would have been present if she had entered the furnace voluntarily. In any event, to enter the fiery furnace feet first would have required some feat of gymnastics. The coroner, who would earn the nickname "Suicide" Murphy, ruled that it was a clear case of suicide by a woman who had become unbalanced as she was passing menopause. *See* DAVID MEYERS and ELISE MEYERS WALKER, HISTORIC COLUMBUS CRIMES 65-71, 122 (2010).

49. Judge Williams's Findings, No. 24, July 19, 1910.

50. Judge Williams's Findings, July 19, 1910.

At the Hospital

51. *Brutal Murder at Union City*, WATERBURY REPUBLICAN, Sept. 19, 1909.

52. *Twelve Bullets Found in Cullwinski's Body*, NAUGATUCK DAILY NEWS, Sept. 20, 1909.

53. I have referred to Dodds as "Lieutenant" and as "Captain" at different points in the narrative. Dodds was listed as a lieutenant in the 1909–1910 city directories. At some point he was promoted to captain. His obituary stated that he was the first member of the detective division to achieve the rank of captain.

54. This from the summary of the evidence in *State v. Kritchman, et al.*, 84 Conn. 152, 79 A. 75 (1911). The findings of the trial judge report the following: "[A]t the hospital, immediately after signing Exhibit 8, Mitchell was brought into the presence of Kulvinskas, and he was asked 'Is this the man who shot you?' Bronislow [Ben] replied, 'Yes.' Thereupon Mitchell said 'Christ Almighty, I didn't do this, Ben, you know that I didn't do this.' Bronislow replied, 'Yes, you did.'"

55. WATERBURY REPUBLICAN, Sept. 20, 1909.

56. *Jealousy of Rival Motive which Leads to Atrocious Crime*, WATERBURY REPUBLICAN, Sept. 20, 1909.

Police Work

57. *Twelve Bullets Found in Cullwinski's Body*, NAUGATUCK DAILY NEWS, Sept. 20, 1909; *Coroner's Finding in Cullwinski Murder*, NAUGATUCK DAILY NEWS, Sept. 21, 1909. *See also Killing Was Most Horrible*, BRIDGEPORT EVENING FARMER, Sept. 21, 1909.

58. *Jealousy of Rival Motive Which Leads to Atrocious Crime*, WATERBURY REPUBLICAN, Sept. 20, 1909; *Jealousy Cause of Saloon Man's Murder*, BRIDGEPORT EVENING FARMER, Sept. 20, 1909; *Murder Caused by Jealousy*, ALEXANDRIA (DC) GAZETTE, Sept. 21, 1909.

59. There was some mention early on in the investigation that Kulvinskas had showed Sophie a roll of bills on Friday morning. WATERBURY REPUBLICAN, Sept. 19, 1909.

60. *Sophia Kritchman Confesses Plot to Murder Kulvinski—Inquest Nearly Completed. Police Seek Eyewitness to Tragedy—Accused Woman Breaks Down—Insanity Is Expected to Be Pleas of Defense—Victim Is Buried*, WATERBURY REPUBLICAN, Sept. 21, 1909; *Coroner Holds Man and Woman for Homicide—Finding of Official Places Criminal Responsibility on Both—Mitchell May Rely on Alibi—Insanity Plea Expected from Kritchmen* [sic] *Woman*, WATERBURY REPUBLICAN, Sept. 22, 1909; *Alibi May Be Relied upon by Mitchell—No Evidence Yet Produced to Connect Lover of Sophie with Crime—Defense Thought to Have Good Case*, WATERBURY REPUBLICAN, Sept. 27, 1909; *Sophia Kritchman Confessed Her Crime*, NORWICH (CONN.) BULLETIN, Sept. 21, 1909.

61. *Twelve Bullets Found in Cullwinski's Body*, NAUGATUCK DAILY NEWS, Sept. 20, 1909.

62. *Trying Woman for Murder*, THE HARTFORD COURANT, Jan. 26, 1910; *Brutal Murder at Union City*, WATERBURY REPUBLICAN, Sept. 19, 1909.

63. *Girl Placed on Trial for Life, Jokes*, PITTSBURGH PRESS, Jan. 27, 1910.

64. *Williamson v. United States*, 512 U.S. 594 (1994). As Justice Sandra Day

O'Connor noted in her opinion, "[One] of the most effective ways to lie is to mix falsehood with truth, especially truth that seems particularly persuasive because of its self-inculpatory nature."

65. WATERBURY REPUBLICAN, Sept. 20, 1909.

66. WATERBURY REPUBLICAN, Sept. 20, 1909; *Love Letters from Doctor*, WATERBURY REPUBLICAN, Sept. 26, 1909.

67. *Music Teacher Held for Murder*, NORWICH BULLETIN, Sept. 20, 1909.

68. *Id.*

69. *Jealousy Cause of Saloon Man's Murder*, BRIDGEPORT EVENING FARMER, Sept. 20, 1909.

70. *Romantic Love Affair, Girl Held for Murder*, THE HARTFORD COURANT, Dec. 30, 1909; *Cupid Enters Jail—Carries Missives from Chicago Doctor to Woman Accused of Naugatuck Murder*, NORWICH BULLETIN, Jan. 5, 1910.

71. *See* NAUGATUCK DAILY NEWS, Sept. 20 and 21, 1909; *Witness Identifies Joe Mitchel As Man with Sophie—Woman's Damaging Testimony Against the Accused at Murder Trial Today*, BRIDGEPORT EVENING FARMER, Mar. 8, 1910.

72. WATERBURY REPUBLICAN, Sept. 21, 1909, and NAUGATUCK DAILY NEWS, Sept. 20 and 21, 1909.

73. *Music Teacher Held for Murder…Sensational Developments—Sophia Kritchman, Lithuanian Music Teacher Figures in a Crime of Which Jealousy Was the Motive*, NORWICH BULLETIN, Sept. 20, 1909.

74. *Jealousy of Rival Motive Which Leads to Atrocious Crime—Ten-Year-Old Child Is Chief Witness Against Pretty Music Teacher Charged with Murder of Bronick Kulivinski—Mary Pokes, Fiancé of Victim, Tells of Her Fears—Local Bartender Said to Have Fired Shot at Instigation of the Woman—She Returns to Poke Body with Stick, Then Buys Revolver to Finish Murder—Mysterious Woman Is Witness—Was Lured to Death by Former Mistress—Revolting Details of Crime*, WATERBURY REPUBLICAN, Sept. 20, 1909.

75. *Jealousy of Rival Motive Which Leads to Atrocious Crime*, WATERBURY REPUBLICAN, Sept. 20, 1909; *Murdered by Rival with Woman's Help*, THE HARTFORD COURANT, Sept. 20, 1909; *Took Girl to See Victim—Child Says Miss Kritchman Found Man Alive and Threatened Her*, N.Y. TIMES, SEPT. 20, 1909.

76. Two witnesses told that Sophie had asked to borrow five dollars and finally got the loan from a Union City woman, and it was believed that she had bought the pistol with the money. WATERBURY REPUBLICAN, Sept. 21, 1909.

77. *Id.*

78. *Id.*

79. *First Degree Murder*, THE HARTFORD COURANT, Sept. 24, 1909; *Grand Jury Finds True Bill*, NAUGATUCK DAILY NEWS, Sept. 23, 1909; *See also Culwinski Murder Case—Will Be Taken Up by Grand Jury Tomorrow Morning in Waterbury—Degrees of Murder Explained by Court*, NAUGATUCK DAILY NEWS, Sept. 22, 1909.

80. *Board of Parole Refuses Pardon to Sophie Kritchman*, THE HARTFORD COURANT, Sept. 4, 1919.

81. *Id.*

82. THE HARTFORD COURANT, Jan. 26, 1910.

83. WATERBURY REPUBLICAN, Sept. 20, 1909.

84. WATERBURY REPUBLICAN, Sept. 21, 1909.

85. *Alleged Murderess Insane?—Sophie Kritchman, Charged with Killing a Friend Acts Strangely—Very Indifferent—and Apparently Lacks Realization of Enormity of Crime*, MERIDEN MORNING RECORD, Sept. 24, 1909.

86. THE STAR (Seattle, WA), Oct. 6, 1909.

87. *What Prompted the Murder?...Post Cards Bearing a Photograph of Sophia Are the Latest*, NAUGATUCK DAILY NEWS, Sept. 25, 1909.

Part Two: The First Trial Begins

The Curtain Rises

88. *Sophia Plans for the Stage—Young Woman Accused of Brutal Murder Considering Vaudeville Offer—Trial to Be Next Week—Prisoner Is Confident She Will Be Acquitted in Superior Court*, WATERBURY REPUBLICAN, Jan. 16, 1910.

89. *Girl, Placed on Trial for Life, Jokes—Pretty Sophia Kritchman, Accused of Brutal Murder, Does Not Seem to Fear Outcome*, Pittsburgh Press, Jan. 27, 1910.

90. *Women Who Died on Gallows in Connecticut—New London County Hanged Girl of Less Than 12 years*, Bridgeport Evening Farmer, Jan. 31, 1910.

91. *Sophie Tells All about Her Love Letters*, Waterbury Republican, Jan. 26, 1910.

92. *Trying Woman for Murder*, and *Sophie Kritchman, the Accused, Smiles at the Proceedings—Looks the Part of a Simple School Girl*, The Hartford Courant, Jan. 26, 1910.

93. *Sophia Plans for the Stage*, Waterbury Republican, Jan. 18, 1910.

94. *See* Richard H. Underwood, Gaslight Lawyers (2017).

95. Pittsburgh Press, Jan. 27, 1910.

96. *Sophia Kritchman's Plea in Murder Case Will Be 'Not Guilty'*, Waterbury Republican, Jan. 23, 1910.

97. *Mitchell Had Key to Trunk in Case—Sophie Told Friend on Night of Murder She Was Going to Marry Mitchell*, The Day (New London, CT), Mar. 3, 1910.

98. Waterbury Republican, Jan. 23, 1910.

99. Waterbury Republican, Jan. 26, 1910.

100. *Id.*

101. *Id.*

102. *Id.*

Sophie in the Dock

103. Waterbury Republican, Jan. 27, 1910.

104. *Id.*; *see also* Naugatuck Daily News, Jan. 27, 1910.

105. Waterbury Republican, Jan. 27, 1910.

106. *Id.*

107. *Id.*

108. *Id.* One wonders if perhaps Kennedy should not have asked Dr. Crane this question but instead should have guided the jurors to draw that conclusion in his summation or closing argument.

109. *Id.*

The Bloody Note

110. *Sophia Kritchman Scores as Witness against an Expert*, WATERBURY REPUBLICAN, Jan. 28, 1910; *Bloody Note Is the Silent Accuser*, NAUGATUCK DAILY NEWS, Jan. 27, 1910.

111. *Sophie Kritchman in Cheerful Mood…Expects Soon to Be Free*, NORWICH BULLETIN, Feb. 3, 1910.

112. *Bloody Note Is Excluded—Important Point Scored in Favor of Sophie Kritchman—Accused Testifies in Clear Loud Voice—And Weeps as Story of Home Life Is Told*, THE HARTFORD COURANT, Jan. 28, 1910.

113 *Sophie Kritchman on Trial*, NORWICH BULLETIN, Jan. 28, 1910.

114. *Sophia Kritchman Scores as Witness Against an Expert*, WATERBURY REPUBLICAN, Jan. 28, 1910.

115. *Id.*

116. *Id.*

117. *Id.*

118. *Id.*

119. *Id.*

120. *Sophie Kritchman on Trial*, NORWICH BULLETIN, Jan. 28, 1910.

121. *Sophia Kritchman Scores as Witness Against an Expert—Denies Handwriting of Blood-Smeared Note Is That of Murdered Man—Exposes Flaw in Interpreter's Translation and Smiles Triumphantly When Court Rules against Paper as Dying Declaration—Weeps When Anton Kulvinskas Is Called and Is on Verge of Hysterics When Session Closes*, WATERBURY REPUBLICAN, Jan. 28, 1910.

122. *'Sophie, I Die at Your Hands'—Last Words of Murdered Man Accuse Music Teacher on Trial as His Slayer*, BRIDGEPORT EVENING FARMER, Jan. 27, 1910.

123. *Id. See also Bloody Note Is the Silent Accuser*, NAUGATUCK DAILY NEWS, Jan. 27, 1910.

Dying Declarations

124. *Prosecution Scores Strong Point against Sophia When Dying Statement Is Admitted—Declaration of Kulvinskas That She Murdered Him, Made to Friend When Found in Woods, Goes before Jury and Prisoner's Confidence Receives Severe Jolt—'Wait until I Tell My Story,' She Pleads—Bitter Contest between Counsel over Every Utterance Offered as Evidence—Court Stenographer on Stand—Doctors Testify as to Weak Mental Condition of Victim at Hospital When Being Examined*, WATERBURY REPUBLICAN, Jan. 29, 1910; *Trying Day for Kritchman—but She Stands It Remarkably Well and Shows Great Confidence in Her Attorney—'Wait until I Tell My Story' She Says*, NAUGATUCK DAILY NEWS, Jan. 29, 1910. See also, *Court Admits Dying Declarations*, NAUGATUCK DAILY NEWS, Jan. 28, 1910.

125. *Will Mitchell Turn State's Evidence in Kritchman Trial*, WATERBURY REPUBLICAN, Jan. 30, 1910; *How Old Is Miss Sophia Kritchman*, NAUGATUCK DAILY NEWS, Jan. 31, 1910.

126. *Prosecution Scores Strong Point against Sophia When Dying Statement Is Admitted...*, WATERBURY REPUBLICAN, Jan. 29, 1910. We are also reminded by this exchange that on cross-examination one should not ask a question to which one does not know the answer.

127. *Id.*

128. Cross-examination of Dr. Crane also brought out that some of the questions to and answers given by Kulvinskas were not in the paper record read by the prosecuting attorney. *See Prosecution Scores in Kritchman Trial—Judge Admits as Evidence More of Kulvinskas' Dying Declaration—But Defense Gained a Point To-Day*, NAUGATUCK DAILY NEWS, Feb. 1, 1910.

129. WATERBURY REPUBLICAN, Jan. 29, 1910.

130. *Prosecution Again Scores Heavily, Kulvinskas' Statement in Hospital Admitted*, THE HARTFORD COURANT, Feb. 2, 1910.

131. *Gruesome Dying Statement of Murdered Man Admitted to Evidence in Waterbury*, BRIDGEPORT EVENING FARMER, Feb. 1, 1910.

132. *Dying Declaration Admitted as Evidence*, NORWICH BULLETIN, Jan. 29, 1910.

133. *Sophia Kritchman Happy When Court Adjourns for Day*, WATERBURY REPUBLICAN, FEB. 3, 1910.

134. *Sophia Kritchman May Tell Her Story to the Jury Today—State Closes Its Case with Strong Web of Circumstantial Evidence Enmeshing Former Union City Music Teacher—Line of Defense Partially Disclosed during Opening Brush between Counsel—Prisoner Shows Much Nervousness—Insanity Experts in Courtroom*, WATERBURY REPUBLICAN, Feb. 4, 1910.

135. THE MERIDEN MORNING RECORD (Meriden, CT), Feb. 2, 1910

136. *Id.* It should be noted that this seems like a bizarre admission—one too good to be true?

137. *Sophia Kritchman Happy When Court Adjourns for Day—Pleased with Counsel's Success in Confusing State's Best Witnesses, Girl Accused of Murder Laughs Heartily at McDermott's Unconventional Testimony—Sister Made Ill by Strain—State May Close Today—No Plea of Insanity is Considered, Atty Kennedy Declares—Prosecutor Presents More Who Saw Prisoner Day of Murder*, WATERBURY REPUBLICAN, Feb. 3, 1910; *Had to Laugh, Says Sophie Kritchman*, THE HARTFORD COURANT, Feb. 3, 1910. *See also States Testimony Is Nearly All In*, NAUGATUCK DAILY NEWS, Feb. 2, 1910. ("[In his examination of Schneer] [e]vidently Attorney Kennedy was making the point that it was apparent from the way he showed Sophia how to shoot and the way he pulled the trigger himself that if Sophia pulled the trigger according to his instructions, she could not have fired shots in quick succession, but would have stopped between shots to pull back the hammer.")

138. *Trial of Sophie Kritchman—State Yesterday Presented Much Damaging Testimony*, NORWICH BULLETIN, Feb. 2, 1910.

139. *Id. See also Defense Begun in Kritchman Trial*, NAUGATUCK DAILY NEWS, Feb. 3, 1910. ("The defense scored another important point by getting excluded from the jury the vital part of the testimony of Walter Roberts… Attorney Kennedy wanted to know why he had not made that statement before the coroner the day following and the witness replied that he could not remember. He also stated that he had not

told all that he knew about the case to the coroner because he had not been asked. Attorney Kennedy asked that his testimony relative to his conversation with Kulvinskas be excluded from the jury on the ground that it was hearsay testimony and that it was not a dying declaration, and also on the ground that the statement was unreliable and not creditable in view of the fact that he had not made the statement before the coroner. After a short recess, Judge Curtis decided to exclude the testimony.") I suspect that some judges would have let the testimony in for what the jury thought it was worth.

140. See sources at note 137.

141. *Id. See also State's Testimony Is Nearly All In...Mrs. John McDermott Cross-Examined More than Two Hours at Morning Session*, Naugatuck Daily News, Feb. 2, 1910; *Atty Kennedy Rattles State Witness Today*, Bridgeport Evening Farmer, Feb. 2, 1910.

142. Norwich Bulletin, Feb. 4, 1910.

143. *Had to Laugh, Says Sophie Kritchman—One of the Happiest Days since Her Arrest—Alleged Dying Statement by Slain Man Rule[d] Out*, The Hartford Courant, Feb. 3, 1910.

144. *Sophia Kritchman Happy When Court Adjourns for Day*, Waterbury Republican, Feb. 3, 1910.

145. The Hartford Courant, Feb. 2, 1910.

146. *Confessions of Dying Man Taken as Evidence*, Los Angeles Herald, Feb. 2, 1910.

147. *Will Mitchell Turn State's Evidence in Kritchman Trial*, Waterbury Republican, Jan. 30, 1910; *How Old Is Miss Sophia Kritchman*, Naugatuck Daily News, Jan. 30, 1910.

148. The Hartford Courant, Jan. 29, 1910.

149. Waterbury Republican, Jan. 30, 1910.

The Defense Opens

150. *Id.*

151. *Sophia Kritchman May Tell Her Story to the Jury Today—State Closes Its Case with Strong Web of Circumstantial Evidence Enmeshing Former Union City Music Teacher—Line of Defense Partially Disclosed during Opening Brush between Counsel—Prisoner Shows Much Nervousness—Insanity Experts in Courtroom*, WATERBURY REPUBLICAN, Feb. 4, 1910; *Music Teacher on Trial for Murder Growing Nervous*, BRIDGEPORT EVENING FARMER, Feb. 4, 1910); *Sophie Kritchman Breaks Down—Worried by Crowd in Court Room She Becomes Almost Hysterical Not Afraid of Lawyers or Jury—But Could Not Stand the Gaze of a Crowd of Women Curiosity Seekers—Hopes the Female Spectators Will Be Kept Out of Court Today—Agrees to Tell the Story of a Quarrel between Two Men for Her Love*, NORWICH BULLETin, Feb. 4, 1910.

152. BRIDGEPORT EVENING FARMER, Feb. 2 and Feb. 3, 1910.

153. *Accused Girl Fears Own Sex More than Law—Sophie Kritchman Faces Charge of Murder, but Quails before Women*, PITTSBURGH POST-GAZETTE, Feb. 4, 1910. *See also Dress Worries Girl at Murder Trial—Sophia Kritchman Fears Women Will Criticise* [sic] *Fit of Her Dress on Stand*, PITTSBURGH DAILY POST, Feb. 4, 1910.

154. Harry Thaw, heir to a $40 million fortune, shot to death architect Stanford White during the performance of a play on the roof garden of Madison Square Garden (which White had designed). The motive for the murder was that White had seduced Evelyn Nesbit, who had afterward married Thaw. Nesbit was only sixteen years old when the statutory rape occurred. Nesbit became an actress, model, and "it girl." Thaw was tried twice. His lawyer Delphin Delmas came up with a theory of temporary insanity and presented a number of experts, including Dr. Britton Evans of the New Jersey State Asylum. He testified that Thaw had had a "severe brain storm." This was a way for Delmas to get in evidence that would allow him to get the *Unwritten Law* (disparage the victim as a seducer and beast, which is not a legal defense). The public was incredulous. Comics called the alienists/psychiatrists "cerebral meteorologists," and a "Brain-Storm Rag" was composed for the piano. *See* Dr. Emil R. Pinta, *The Murder Trials of Harry K. Thaw (1907 and 1908) and Dr. Arthur Waite (1916) and The Perplexing Concept of 'Constitutional Infirmity'*, (Ohio Academy of Medical History, Apr. 13, 2013) at http://corescholar.libraries.wright.edu/oamh_presentations/3 (last visited June 6, 2025). Dr. Diefendorf was an expert for the prosecution. He testified that Thaw may have been medically insane, but he was legally responsible because he was able to determine right from wrong and knew the nature of his act. Dr. Diefendorf was the superinten-

dent of the Connecticut General Hospital for the Insane at Middletown, where Sophie would reside for a short time after her conviction. The reader may know that Evelyn Nesbit was famous—or infamous—as *The Girl in the Red Velvet Swing.*

155. *Weak Mentality Kritchman Defense,* The Hartford Courant, Feb. 4, 1910.

156. *Id.*

157. *Id.*

158. *Id.*

159. *Experts Battle in Kritchman Trial—Was Victim Fit to Make Coherent Statements?,* The Hartford Courant, Feb. 5, 1910.

160. One is reminded of the "bloody glove don't fit" sideshow in the O. J. Simpson trial. *See* Vincent Bugliosi, Outrage 143-146 (1996).

161. *Sophie Kritchman on Witness Stand,* Naugatuck Daily News, Feb. 4, 1910.

162. *Id.*

163. The Hartford Courant, Feb. 5, 1910.

164. *Trial of Mitchell and Sophie Resumed: Dying Statement of Kulvinskas Is Admitted,* The Hartford Courant, Mar. 1, 1910.

165. *Document to Convict Girl?—Text of Dying Statement of Kulvinskas State's Chief Weapon against Sophia—Experts Differ on It—Full Text as Reported by Stenographer of Court—Man's Queer Answers,* Waterbury Republican, Feb. 6, 1910.

166. Dodds was a detective, later promoted to lieutenant and then captain. He was apparently the first detective to achieve the rank of captain.

167. *Music Teacher on Trial for Murder Growing Nervous,* Bridgeport Evening Farmer, Feb. 4, 1910. Bridgeport Evening Farmer, Feb. 4, 1910, reported that that O'Brien was "positive that any statement Kulvinskas might have made was not intelligible enough to have been understood by the authorities on the scene. This…was in direct contradiction of previous statements made by the state's witnesses to the effect that Kulvinskas had clearly implicated Sophia and Mitchell as his slayers."

168. *Sophia's Trial May Last Another Week—Legal Battle Over Expert Testimony Is Expected to Take a Few Days—Sophia Is Confident of Acquittal,* NAUGATUCK DAILY NEWS, Feb. 5, 1910; *Experts Plan for Stiff Battle over Dying Declaration,* WATERBURY REPUBLICAN, Feb. 5, 1910. *Third Week of Murder Trial…Medical Experts Will Be Heard This Week…Big Legal Battle Will Take Place over Testimony of the Experts,* NAUGATUCK DAILY NEWS, Feb. 7, 1910.

Mistrial

169. *Sophia Gets Letter with Death Threat—Extra Deputy Sheriff to Be Added to Guards—Text of Missive—Medical Experts to Go On Stand Today,* WATERBURY REPUBLICAN, Feb. 8, 1910.

170. *Threatens to Kill Kritchman Girl—Letter Warns Her against Accusing Joe Mitchell of Murder,* THE HARTFORD COURANT, Feb. 8, 1910.

171. *Id. See also Threatened Sophie Kritchman,* NORWICH BULLETIN, Feb. 8, 1910.

172. *Jury in Murder Trial Is Dismissed by Judge Howard J. Curtis Today,* BRIDGEPORT EVENING FARMER, Feb. 8, 1910.

173. *Publication of Letter Ends Kritchman Trial—Dismissal of Jury and Removal of Counsel for the Defense,* THE HARTFORD COURANT, Feb. 8, 1910.

174. *Id. See also Mistrial Due to Lawyer Kennedy's Act,* NORWICH BULLETIN, Feb. 9, 1910.

175. *Jury in Sophia Kritchman's Trial Discharged This Morning,* NAUGATUCK DAILY NEWS, Feb. 8, 1910.

176. *Sophie Kritchman's New Trial,* NAUGATUCK DAILY NEWS, Feb. 9, 1910.

177. Records of the Superior Court: "Plea of former jeopardy and motion for discharge," Feb. 11, 1910; "Replication to plea of former jeopardy (etc.)," Feb. 14, 1910; "State's Demurer to portions of replication," Feb. 14, 1910; "Answer to Replication," Feb. 14, 1910.

178. *Asks to Have Sophie Discharged,* NAUGATUCK DAILY NEWS, Feb. 11, 1910; *Motion for Discharge of Sophia Kritchman—Will Be Argued in Superior Court Monday Afternoon,* NAUGATUCK DAILY NEWS, Feb. 12, 1910. One assumes that this would have been an issue in any appeal by Sophie if she

were convicted. In the end, it appears that she did not pursue an appeal—but more on that later.

179. Records of the Superior Court: "Judgment on Plea of Former Jeopardy, by Williams, J.," Feb. 14, 1910; "Memorandum of Decision—denying plea of former jeopardy."

180. *New Kritchman Trial to Begin Tuesday*, THE HARTFORD COURANT, Feb. 12, 1910.

181. *Motion for Joint Trial of Sophia and Mitchell*, NAUGATUCK DAILY NEWS, Feb. 10, 1910; *Asks to Have Sophia Discharged…Arguments on State's Motion for Joint Trial*, NAUGATUCK DAILY NEWS, Feb. 11, 1910; *Motion in Sophia's Case*, NAUGATUCK DAILY NEWS, Feb. 14, 1910; *Selecting Jurors for Murder Trial…Sophia and Mitchell to Be Tried Together*, NAUGATUCK DAILY NEWS, Feb. 15, 1910.

182. Records of the Superior Court: "Further Objection to the Impanelling of the Jury," Feb. 15, 1910; "Objection of Sophis [sic] Kritchman to Order for Joint Trial", Feb. 18, 1910.

183. A "cut throat defense is when the State…tries to convict two people of the same crime. And then you have got the two defendants over there saying that the other did it. In other words [Defendant One] is going to testify over there that [Defendant Two] was the one that committed the crime, and vice versa." *Ex parte Tommy Washington v. State of Alabama*, 562 So. 2d 1304 (Ala. 1990).

184. *State v. Howell*, 80 Conn. 668, 69 A. 1057 (1908). *Law Set Forth to the Newspapers—Abstract of the Howell Case Quoted in the Kritchman Trial*, THE HARTFORD COURANT, Feb. 16, 1910; *Law Set Forth to the Newspapers—Abstract of the Howell Case Quoted in the Kritchman Trial*, BRIDGEPORT EVENING FARMER, Feb. 17, 1910. In case the reader is wondering, in 1910 the First Amendment had not yet been held applicable to the states.

Part Three: Joint Trial

Joint Trial Opens

185. *Kritchman Girl and Mitchell on Trial—First Day Spent in Endeavor to Get*

Jurors, Feb. 16, 1910; *New Panel of Fifty Chosen for Trial of Music Teacher*, Bridgeport Evening Farmer, Feb. 16, 1910.

186. *Bloody Evidence Produced in Court—Jury Is Completed in Mitchell-Kritchman Trial*, Feb. 19, 1910. *See also Seven Jurors Have Been Selected*, Naugatuck Daily News, Feb. 16, 1910; *Jury Panel Exhausted Today*, Naugatuck Daily News, Feb. 17, 1910.

187. *Special Cell for Mob Scared Pal of Sophia*, Bridgeport Times and Evening Farmer, Feb. 17, 1910.

188. *Tenth Juror to Try Sophia Kritchmen*, Bridgeport Evening Farmer, Feb. 18, 1910.

189. *New Panel of 50 Chosen for Trial of Music Teacher*, Bridgeport Evening Farmer, Feb. 16, 1910.

190. *Taking of Testimony Begun This Afternoon*, Naugatuck Daily News, Feb. 18, 1910.

191. *Id.*

192. *Id.*

193. *Juror's Illness Delays Trial*, Naugatuck Daily News, Feb. 22, 1910; *Trial Postponed by Juror's Illness—Kritchman-Mitchell Case Goes over until Monday*, Naugatuck Daily News, Feb. 23, 1910.

194. *Witnesses Say Dead Man Accused Sophie Kritchman*, Bridgeport Evening Farmer, Mar. 4, 1910.

195. *Id. See also First Week of Murder Trial*, Naugatuck Daily News, Feb. 22, 1910.

196. *Murder Trial from Waterbury to New Haven*, Bridgeport Evening Farmer, Mar. 2, 1910. *Kulvinskas Case Obliged to Move—Waterbury Court House to Be Replaced So Trial Is Taken to New Haven*, Naugatuck Daily News, Mar. 2, 1910; *Photographs Shown to Jury*, Naugatuck Daily News, Mar. 1, 1910.

197. *Talesmen Summoned, Kritchman Jury Box Filled*, Norwich Bulletin, Feb. 19, 1910.

198. *Sophie Nervous at Murder Trial—Young Music Teacher Does Not Like Crowded Court Room in New Haven*, Bridgeport Evening Farmer, Mar. 3, 1910.

199. *Trial of Mitchell and Sophie Resumed*, THE HARTFORD COURANT, Mar. 1, 1910.

200. *Jury Hears Dying Declaration—Statement Made by Bronislaw Kulvinskas to Prosecuting Attorney McGrath Read by State Attorney Alling*, NAUGATUCK DAILY NEWS, Feb. 28, 1910.

201. *Change in Victoria Dalton's Testimony*, NAUGATUCK DAILY NEWS, Mar. 2, 1910.

202. *Photographs Shown to Jury*, NAUGATUCK DAILY NEWS, Mar. 1, 1910.

203. *Court Admits More Dying Declarations*, NAUGATUCK DAILY NEWS, Mar. 7, 1910.

204. *Change in Victoria Dalton's Testimony—She Declared To-day That It Was Not a Garter That She Saw Sophia Take from Her Stocking*, NAUGATUCK DAILY NEWS, Mar. 2, 1910.

205. *Child Who Was with Sophie Testifies—Took Something Black and Shiny from Stocking—Saw Her Go into Bushes and Heard Shouting*, THE HARTFORD COURANT, Mar. 3, 1910.

206. *Id. See also Trial Being Held in New Haven—State Is Making Rapid Progress in Case of Sophie Kritchman and Joseph Mitchell To-day*, NAUGATUCK DAILY NEWS, May 3, 1910.

207. Assuming that Kennedy had impeached Victoria Dalton's testimony with prior inconsistent testimony in the previous trial, her earlier prior consistent statements made during the investigation may have been admissible on redirect for the purpose of repairing any damage to her credibility. The newspaper accounts make no mention of any attempt by Alling to use her original statements to the police about a razor, but he may very well have. For her early mention of a knife or razor, *see Jealousy of Rival Motive Which Leads to Atrocious Crime*, WATERBURY REPUBLICAN, Sept. 20, 1909.

208. *Kulvinskas's Brother Testifies*, THE HARTFORD COURANT, Mar. 4, 1910.

209. *Trial Being Held in New Haven*, NAUGATUCK DAILY NEWS, Mar. 3, 1910.

210. *Dying Declarations; Blood Stained Note—Testimony Relative to Their Admissibility Has Occupied a Part of To-days Trial—Jury Excused While Testimony Was Presented*, NAUGATUCK DAILY NEWS, Mar. 4, 1910.

211. *Mitchell Had Key to Trunk in Case—Sophie Told Friend on Night of Murder She Was Going to Marry Mitchell*, THE DAY (New London, CT), Mar. 3, 1910.

212. *Blood Stained Note Admitted as Evidence*, THE HARTFORD COURANT, Mar. 4, 1910; *Blood Stained Note Admitted to Jury*, NAUGATUCK DAILY NEWS, Mar. 5, 1910. (Judge Williams would not admit as dying declarations the statements made by Kulvinskas to Joseph Pecukewiez, Joseph Noerkewiez, and Joseph Raykiewich.) *Bloodstained Note Admitted as Evidence*, NORWICH BULLETIN, Mar. 5, 1910. *But see Witnesses Say Dead Man Accused Sophie Kritchman*, BRIDGEPORT EVENING FARMER, Mar. 4, 1910, which reports that M.R. Malinowsky's translation of the letter was excluded by Judge Williams.

213. *Court Admits More Dying Declaration—Chief of Police Schmidt Heard Kulvinskas Say Sophia Kritchman and Joe Mitchell 'Killed' Him*, NAUGATUCK DAILY NEWS, Mar. 7, 1910; *State Rests in Kritchman Trial— The Dying Man's Statements Accusing Girl Admitted*, THE HARTFORD COURANT, Mar. 7, 1910; *Murder Trial of Sophie and Joe Mitchell on Today*, BRIDGEPORT EVENING FARMER, Mar. 7, 1910; *State Rests in Kritchman Murder Case—Evidence of Closing Scores Telling Points against Music Teacher—Defense Will Open Case This Morning*, WATERBURY REPUBLICAN, Mar. 8, 1910.

214. *State Rests in Kritchman Murder Case—Evidence of Closing Scores Telling Points against Music Teacher—Defense Will Open this Morning*, WATERBURY REPUBLICAN, MAR. 8, 1910.

215. *Id.*

216. *Id.*

217. *Id.*

218. *Defense in Murder Trial Begun*, WATERBURY REPUBLICAN, Mar. 8, 1910.

219. *Id.*

220. *Dying Declaration; Blood Stained Note*, NAUGATUCK DAILY NEWS, Mar. 4, 1910.

221. *Id.*

222. *Sophie Kritchman Case, State Rests*, NORWICH BULLETIN, Mar. 8, 1910; *State Rests in Trial of Sophie Kritchman*, THE MORNING CALL (Allentown, PA), Mar. 8, 1910.

Sophie Tells Her Story

223. *Point Scored for Sophia in Her Defense—Alleged Motive Brought Out in Kritchman Trial Counts against Mitchell—Witness Tells of Fight between Men*, WATERBURY REPUBLICAN, Mar. 9, 1910.

224. *Id. See also Defense in Murder Trial Begun*, NAUGATUCK DAILY NEWS, Mar. 4, 1910.

225. *Id.*

226. *Id. See also Kritchman Defense in Murder Trial Begun—Fight between Kulvinskas and Mitchell Described*, THE HARTFORD COURANT, Mar. 9, 1910; *Evidence Points Strongly to Guilt of Joe Mitchell—His Quarrel with Kulvinskas and Bad Blood Long Existing between Them and Sophie's Friendly Relations with Dead Man Emphasized*, THE DAY (New London, CT) May 9, 1910. *Lengthy Examination of Witnesses—Mrs. Nellie Antonaitis Testified that Joe Had Said that If Bronislaw Did Not Keep Away from Sophia, He Would Be Carried Out of 'The City' Like a Dead Dog…*, NAUGATUCK DAILY NEWS, Mar. 9, 1910; *First Day Of Kritchman Defense—Two Entirely New and Important Pieces of Testimony Were Brought Out—Mitchell and Kulvinskas in Scrap Quarrel Took Place in Yard of Sophie's House the Night Preceding the Shooting of Kulvinskas—Mitchell Positively Identified for the First Time as Having Been Seen near Locality of the Crime*, NORWICH BULLETIN, Mar. 9, 1910.

227. *Point Scored for Sophia in Her Defense—Alleged Motive Brought Out in Kritchman Trial Counts Against Mitchell—Witness Tells of Fight Between Men*, WATERBURY REPUBLICAN, Mar. 9, 1910.

228. *Miss Kritchman Will Unfold Her Story of the Union City Murder—Accused Music Teacher Expected to Go on Stand in New Haven Today—Sister Tells of Mitchell's Threat, Second Identification of Man Claiming Alibi Surprises Counsel*, WATERBURY REPUBLICAN, Mar. 10, 1910.

229. *Id.*

230. *Id. See also Sophia Testifies in Her Own Defense*, NAUGATUCK DAILY NEWS, Mar. 10, 1910.

231. *Id.*

232. *Afraid of Mitchell Says Accused Girl—Girl's Fiancé, from Chicago—Sits beside Her in Court*, THE HARTFORD COURANT, Mar. 15, 1910; *To Accused*

Fiancée's Aid—Dr. Rutzkaukas Meets Sophie Kritchman for First Time at Murder Trial, N.Y. TIMES, Mar. 15, 1910.

233. *Sophia Weds If Innocent in Jury's Eye—Dr. Rutkauskas, Her Lover, in Court Tells of Their Strange Courtship—Newspaper Story Arouses Interest*, WATERBURY REPUBLICAN, Mar. 15, 1910.

234. *Unwritten Law May Be Invoked in Trial*, WATERBURY REPUBLICAN, Mar. 11, 1910.

235. *Kritchman Girl Lays Blame on Mitchell—Her Story of Killing of Kulvinskas—Breaks Down Several Times When Testifying—Says Shots Were Fired as They Sat Together*, THE HARTFORD COURANT, Mar. 11, 1910; *Sophie Kritchman Breaks Down under An All Day Merciless Fire of Questions from Prosecutor Kellogg Spectators Made Her Very Nervous—Sophie Continued Her Story of the Killing of Kulvinskas, Telling in Detail the Shooting of the Wounded Victim by Mitchell and of the Latter Threatening to Kill Her If She Told—Courtroom Crowded*, NORWICH BULLETIN, Mar. 12, 1910.

236. *Id. See also Miss Kritchman's Session in Witness Box Is Concluded*, WATERBURY REPUBLICAN, Mar. 15, 1910. The article refers to the "salacious testimony."

237. *Unwritten Law May Be Invoked in Trial—Sophia Kritchman Tells Dramatic Story of Murder of Bronislaw Kulvinskas Following Attempted Assault—Accuses Mitchell of Firing the Fatal Shots—Girl Takes Stand in Her Own Defense*, WATERBURY REPUBLICAN, Mar. 11, 1910; *Miss Kritchman on Stand—Says That Mitchell, Accused with Her of Murder, Shot Kulvinskas*, N.Y. TIMES, Mar. 11, 1910; *Sophia Testifies in Her Own Defense*, NAUGATUCK DAILY NEWS, Mar. 10, 1910.

238. *Miss Kritchman's Session in Witness Box Is Concluded*, WATERBURY REPUBLICAN, Mar. 15, 1910.

239. *Love Letters of Girl Are Read to Jurymen in Kritchman Trial—Sophia, Charged with Murder of Bronislaw Kulvinskas, Continues Her Defense—Grilling Cross-Examination by Kellogg—Women Send Girl Candy and Flowers—Could She Pull the Trigger?—Prayed for Kulvinskas*, WATERBURY REPUBLICAN, Mar. 12, 1910. *See also, Sophia: Love Letter to Mitchell*, NAUGATUCK DAILY NEWS, Mar. 11, 1910.

240. *Id.* For similar coverage, see *'I'm Awful Tired,' Sophia Exclaimed*, NAUGATUCK DAILY NEWS, Mar. 12, 1910.

241. *Kritchman Defense May End Tuesday—Is Accused Girl Acting Her Part,* WATERBURY REPUBLICAN, Mar. 13, 1910.

242. *Id.*

243. *Id. See also Sophia's Love Letters to Mitchell,* NAUGATUCK DAILY NEWS, Mar. 11, 1910.

244. WATERBURY REPUBLICAN, MAR. 13, 1910.

245. *Id.*

246. *Sophie's Defense Not Yet Finished,* NAUGATUCK DAILY NEWS, Mar. 14, 1910.

247. *Miss Kritchman's Session in Witness Box Is Concluded,* WATERBURY REPUBLICAN, Mar. 15, 1910.

248. *Expert Testimony Given To-Day—Dr. Diefendorf Expressed Opinion That Kulvinskas Was Unable to Make Accurate Statement—Subjected to Lengthy Cross Examination,* NAUGATUCK DAILY NEWS, Mar. 15, 1910; *Testifies for Music Teacher,* BRIDGEPORT EVENING FARMER, Mar. 16, 1910.

249. *Kritchman Defense Rests and Mitchell Witnesses Testify—Sophia's Chicago Lover Takes Stand in Her Behalf—Medical Experts Called for Girl— Testimony That Defendant Could Not Pull Trigger of Revolver—Mitchell Begins Proof of an Alibi,* WATERBURY REPUBLICAN, Mar. 16, 1910.

250. *Id.*

251. *Testifies for Music Teacher,* BRIDGEPORT EVENING FARMER, Mar. 16, 1910. *Sophie Kritchman Examination Over—Had Been on the Witness Stand Thirteen Hours—Arrival of Her Fiancé from Chicago Seemed to Give Her New Strength—She Was Afraid of Joe Mitchell and His Friends,* NORWICH BULLETIN, Mar. 15, 1910.

252. WATERBURY REPUBLICAN, Mar. 16, 1910; *Closing of Kritchman Defense,* NORWICH BULLETIN, Mar. 16, 1910.

Mitchell's Defense

253. *Mitchell's Witnesses Take Stand—Severe Cross-Examination by Attorney Kennedy—Did Sophia Accuse Another?—Chicago Physician Leaves for His Home,* WATERBURY REPUBLICAN, Mar. 17, 1910.

254. For more coverage of Mitchell's alibi witnesses, see *Joe Mitchell on Witness Stand*, NAUGATUCK DAILY NEWS, Mar. 18, 1910; *Five Witnesses to Prove Alibi for Joe Mitchell*, BRIDGEPORT EVENING FARMER, Mar. 16, 1910; *Alibi Continued for Joe Mitchell, Alleged Murderer*, BRIDGEPORT EVENING FARMER, Mar. 17, 1910.

255. *Id. See also I Don't Remember Witnesses in The Mitchell Defense*, NORWICH BULLETIN, Mar. 17, 1910; *Witnesses Could Not Remember—Joe Mitchell's Friends All Forget at the Proper Time*, RECORD JOURNAL (Meriden, CT), Mar. 18, 1910.

256. *Compare Witnesses Must Speak Louder—Yesterday's Proceedings in Mitchell Defense Dragged Slowly—State May Bring Out Some New Evidence*, NORWICH BULLETIN, Mar. 18, 1910.

257. *Id.*

258. *Id.*

259. *Mitchell's Defense Heard To-Day—Presentation of His Side of the Case Has Taken up Whole Session*, NAUGATUCK DAILY NEWS, Mar. 16, 1910. *See also, Mitchell Tells of His Doings Since Labor Day*, THE NORWICH HOUR, Mar. 18, 1910.

260. *Joe Mitchell Tells Jury Careful Story—Man Accused of Murder of Bronislaw Kulvinskas Completes His Direct Testimony, Goes into Minute Detail—Attorney Lynch Leads Client thru Intricate Maze of Testimony—Defendant Unshaken by State's Attorney*, WATERBURY REPUBLICAN, Mar. 19, 1910; *Mitchell On Stand Today—Denies Sophie's Statements—Tells of Movements*, THE JOURNAL (Meriden, CT), March 18, 1910.

261. *Mitchell Concludes His Story on Stand, Seems Satisfied with his Showing When He Returns to Seat Beside Counsel—Rebuttal Begun and Arguments Will Be Concluded Thursday, Case Going to Jury That Afternoon—Mrs. Bowers Mentioned as Sweetheart of Mitchell, Who Also Acknowledged His Love for Sophia Although Denying That He Proposed to Her*, WATERBURY REPUBLICAN, Mar. 22, 1910. *See also May Go to Jury on Thursday—… Under Fire Eleven Hours—Mitchell Showed Extreme Nervousness—Direct Question Twice Put 'Did You Shoot Kulvinskas?'*, NORWICH BULLETIN, Mar. 22, 1910. *See also, Says He Did Not Shoot Kulvinskas*, NAUGATUCK DAILY NEWS, Mar. 21, 1910.

262. *Mitchell Thought of Marrying Sophia*, NAUGATUCK DAILY NEWS, Mar. 19, 1910.

263. *Mitchell Concludes His Story on Stand*, Waterbury Republican, Mar. 22, 1910.

264. *Id.*

265. *Id. See also Trial of Sophie Kritchman and Joe Mitchell*, Norwich Bulletin, Mar. 4, 1910, which reported that under cross-examination of Attorney Lynch on behalf of Mitchell, Antone had admitted that he had once opened his locked trunk with a knife blade.

266. According to the Jewish Calendar 1909 Diaspora, available at hebcal.com, it was Tishri Rosh Hashana 1 September 16, and Tishri Rosh Hashana 2 September 17.

267. *Arguments in Murder Trial—The Whole of the Morning Session Was Taken up with Testimony in Rebuttal—Judge Williams Refused to Allow Handkerchief Found in Sophia Kritchman's Cell to Be Introduced as Evidence*, Naugatuck Daily News, Mar. 23, 1910.

268. In Mitchell's hearing before the Board of Pardons, Louis Raffel claimed that Prosecutor Alling had said that Weisman's testimony was unreliable and had told the jury to throw it out. *See 3 Life Prisoners among 8 Freed by Board of Pardons*, The Hartford Courant, Dec. 19, 1923. I have not been able to find this statement by Alling in the newspaper coverage of the summations of counsel. If Alling made such a statement, I do not know the context in which it was made. Sometimes lawyers tell jurors to disregard evidence that the other side thinks important, arguing that it does not matter. He may have argued that there was enough evidence to convict Mitchell even without Weisman's testimony.

269. This is interesting to me because the relevant Model Rule of Professional Conduct that most lawyers would look to today, Model Rule 3.3(a)(3), states that a lawyer must take reasonable remedial measures to correct perjury if the testimony has been given by the lawyer's client or a witness called by the lawyer. On the Kritchman facts, the witness was called by Sophie's defense lawyer, so the prosecutors might argue that they had no duty to take any remedial measures; but does that mean that they could rely on testimony they knew was false? I suspect that legal ethics experts would say that the prosecution should not be permitted to do so, although I am not sure what they would say if a defense lawyer engaged in similar conduct.

270. *Testimony of Waterbury Widow—Furnished the Greatest Interest Tuesday in Kritchman Mitchell Trial—Evidence All In—Judge Will Charge Jury on Saturday Morning*, Norwich Bulletin, Mar. 23, 1910.

271. *All Evidence Against Mitchell and Sophia Kritchman Concluded*, WATERBURY REPUBLICAN, Mar. 23, 1910.

272. *Id.*

273. *Arguments in Murder Trial*, NAUGATUCK DAILY NEWS, Mar. 23, 1910.

Closing Arguments

274. WATERBURY REPUBLICAN, Mar. 24, 1910.

275. *Final Arguments for Defense Made in Murder Trial*, WATERBURY REPUBLICAN, Mar. 25, 1910. *Arguments in Murder Trial*, NAUGATUCK DAILY NEWS, Mar. 23, 1910.

276. *Brilliant Plea Made for Life of Kritchman Girl by Sen. Kennedy*, WATERBURY REPUBLICAN, Mar. 24, 1910; BRIDGEPORT EVENING FARMER, Mar. 23, 1910.

277. *Id.*

278. *Eloquent and Dramatic Arguments Heard Today*, NAUGATUCK DAILY NEWS, Mar. 23, 1910.

279. *Id.*

280. *Kritchman-Mitchell Case Nearing the Jury*, NORWICH BULLETIN, Mar. 24, 1910.

281. *Brilliant Plea Made for Life of Kritchman Girl by Sen. Kennedy*, WATERBURY REPUBLICAN, Mar. 24, 1910.

282. *Id.*

283. *Id. See also Sophie Kritchman in Defiant Mood—Sneers at Denouncers during Scathing Arraignment in Closing Arguments of Opposing Counsel*, NORWICH BULLETIN, Mar. 25, 1910.

Jury Instructions

284. Frank Hoyt, *The Judge's Power to Comment on the Testimony in His Charge to the Jury*, 11 MARQ. L. REV. 67 (1927).

285. *Waiting for Verdict in Case of Sophia Kritchman and Joe Mitchell*, Naugatuck Daily News, Mar. 26, 1910.

286. *Judge Made a Lengthy Charge—Sophie Kritchman Moved to Tears by Music*, The Norwalk Hour, Mar. 26, 1910.

287. *Id. See also Kritchman Girl Is Found Guilty*, N.Y. Times, Mar. 27, 1910.

288. *Judge Made a Lengthy Charge—Sophie Kritchman Moved to Tears By Music*, The Norwalk Hour, Mar. 26, 1910; *Jury Out in Celebrated Waterbury Murder Case*, Bridgeport Evening Farmer, Mar. 26, 1910.

Verdict and Sentences

289. *Kritchman Verdict: Sophia Guilty*, Waterbury Republican, Mar. 26, 1910; *Sophie Kritchman and Mitchell Guilty*, The Hartford Courant, Mar. 28, 1910; *Sophie Kritchman Is Convicted*, Norwich Bulletin, Mar. 28, 1910.

290. *Man and Woman Both Guilty*, Sun (N.Y.), Mar. 27, 1910; *Kritchman Girl Found Guilty*, N.Y. Times, Mar. 27, 1910; *Girl Murderer Is Convicted*, Ogden (UT) Morning Examiner, Mar. 27, 1910.

291. *Sentence Is Deferred until Tomorrow after Jury Finds Sophia and Mitchell Guilty—He Remains Silent, Unmoved; She Breaks Down and Weeps Bitterly—Had Been Hopeful to the Last*, Waterbury Republican, March 27, 1910.

292. *Murder Accomplices Sentenced Today*, Barre Daily News (Barre, VT), Mar. 28, 1910; *Kritchman Girl Sentenced*, N.Y. Times, Mar. 29, 1910; *Mitchell Defiant but Sophia Weeps Bitterly When Given Sentence—Former Hears 'for Life' without Flinching—Latter Declares She Won't Live 12 Years—Wishes It Had Been Death—Physician Says Miss Kritchman Has Consumption— Girl Will Join Prison Sewing Dept.—Judge Attacks Witnesses*, Waterbury Republican, Mar. 29, 1910; *Sophia's Condition Said to Be Serious—Miss Kritchman Reported to Be in a State of Coma at the New Haven County Jail—Visited by a Catholic Priest Today—Since the Pronouncement of Her Sentence She Has Been in a Hysterical Condition, but Yesterday She Appeared to be Worse than at Any Time since She Was Taken Ill*, Naugatuck Daily News, Mar. 31, 1910.

293. *Id.*

294. Waterbury Republican, Mar. 29, 1910.

295. *Id. See also Life Imprisonment for Joe Mitchell; Not Less than 12 or More than 15 Years for Sophia Kritchman*, NAUGATUCK DAILY NEWS, Mar. 28, 1910.

296. *See Paresis a Living Death—Dr. Talcott Describes the Scourge That Has Stricken Prominent Men*, WESTMORELAND RECORDER (Westmoreland, KS), Dec. 1, 1887; *All about Paresis—An Insidious Disease Which Destroys Many Brain-Workers*, WAIKATO TIMES (Hamilton, NZ), Dec. 21, 1889; *About Paresis—Five Leading Experts Describe Its Symptoms*, THE BROOKLYN CITIZEN (Brooklyn, NY), Jan. 24, 1892.

297. "At the beginning of the century [twentieth century] there was some debate as to whether all cases of general paresis were due to syphilis. Today there can be no question that all cases of general paresis are the result of an invasion of the brain by the Treponema pallidum. The symptoms generally manifest themselves a decade or more after the syphilitic infection is acquired." MANFRED S. GUTTMACHER AND HENRY WEIHOFEN, PSYCHIATRY AND THE LAW 142 (1952); *Tapping the Skulls of Maniacs to Learn Cause of Paresis*, COURIER-JOURNAL, May 28, 1916; Susan Eyrich Lederer, *The Right And Wrong Of Making Experiments On Human Beings: Udo J. Wile and Syphilis*, 58 BULLETIN OF THE HISTORY OF MEDICINE 380-397 (1984); Emily Vogel, *Perspectives on the Experimentation of Udo J. Wile: Insights into the Past and Considerations for Today*, IV:1 MICHIGAN J. OF HISTORY, Fall 2006 (https://michiganjournalhistory.files.wordpress.com/2014/02/vogel_emily.pdf) (last visited June 6, 2025).

298. *Mitchell Defiant, But Sophie Weeps Bitterly When Given Sentence*, WATERBURY REPUBLICAN, Mar. 29, 1910.

299. *Life Imprisonment for Joe Mitchell; Not Less than 12 or More than 15 Years for Sophia Kritchman*, NAUGATUCK DAILY NEWS, Mar. 28, 1910.

300. *Waiting for Verdict in Case of Sophia Kritchman and Joe Mitchell*, NAUGATUCK DAILY NEWS, Mar. 26, 1910.

301. *Bills for $20,000 in Murder Trial of Sophie Kritchman and Mitchell*, BRIDGEPORT EVENING FARMER, May 24, 1910.

Part Four: Springtime for Sophie

The Appeal

302. 84 Conn. 152 (1911).

303. An April 14, 1910, newspaper article suggested that she would appeal on grounds of double jeopardy, but nothing came of it. *See Sophie Goes to the Supreme Court—Will Appeal on Ground That Her Life Was Twice in Jeopardy*, Bridgeport Evening Farmer, Apr. 14, 1910; *Sophie Kritchman Case—May Be Appealed to Supreme Court of Errors*, Norwich Bulletin, April 14, 1910.

304. *No New Trial for Mitchell—Supreme Court of Errors Denies Appeal of Man Convicted of Murder*, Bridgeport Evening Farmer, Mar. 9, 1911; *New Trial Is Denied by Court*, Norwich Bulletin, Mar. 9, 1911.

305. *Kritchman Murder Case Before Supreme—Appeal of Joe Mitchell, Serving Life Term for Complicity, Argued*, The Hartford Courant, Jan. 18, 1911.

306. *See Brief in Behalf of Joseph, alias Joseph Mitchell*, at 21-22.

Incarceration

307. *Joe Mitchell Taken to Prison*, Naugatuck Daily News, Apr. 1, 1910.

308. *Sophia Kritchman Taken to Prison*, Naugatuck Daily News, Apr. 4, 1910; *Sophie Kritchman Goes to Prison Laughing*, The Hartford Courant, Apr. 15, 1910. This account is in contrast to another, which described her as being inured to the crowd, her face pale and wan as she left the Whalley Avenue jail in New Haven. *Sophie Starts Sentence in Wethersfield Prison*, Bridgeport Evening Farmer, Apr. 5, 1910.

309. *Sophie Kritchman Judged Insane*, The Hartford Courant, Mar. 10, 1911; *Union City Murderess Is Adjudged Insane—Sophie Kritchman Transferred from Prison to the Insane Hospital*, Norwich Bulletin, Mar. 11, 1911.

310. *Sophie Kritchman Wants to Go Home after Prison Life*, The Hartford Courant, July 22, 1919; *Sophie Kritchman Plans to Marry Naugatuck Man—Released from State Prison May 9, Woman Convicted of Murdering Lover, Is to Become Wife of Lithuanian—Was Tennis Champion at State Hospital*, The Hartford Courant, Sept. 27, 1920.

311. James E. Overmeyer, '*Baseball for the Insane': The Middletown State Homeopathic Hospital and Its 'Asylums*,' 19 Nine: A Journal of Baseball History and Culture 27-43 (2011); Jonathan Davidson, A Century of Homeopaths; Their Influence on Medicine and Health 67-68 (2014).

312. *Sophie Kritchman Writes Verse*, THE HARTFORD COURANT, FEB. 11, 1913.

313. © April 7 and 8, 1910, *Sophie Kritchman*, New Haven, Connecticut.

314. © August 14, 1912, *Sophia Kritchman*, Middletown, Connecticut.

315. *Sophie Kritchman Wants to Go Home after Prison Life*, THE HARTFORD COURANT, July 22, 1919.

316. *Sophie Kritchman Wants a Piano—Insane Murderess Plays a Joke on Waterbury Music Dealer*, THE HARTFORD COURANT, Aug. 23, 1912.

317. *Sophie Kritchman Did Not Unloosen Bar*, THE HARTFORD COURANT, Sept. 10, 1913.

318. *Sophie Kritchman Returned to Prison*, THE HARTFORD COURANT, Feb. 14, 1914; *Insane Murderess Back to Prison*, THE HARTFORD COURANT, Feb. 11, 1914; *Wethersfield*, NORWICH BULLETIN, Feb. 17, 1914; *Sophie Kritchman Is Returned to Prison*, BRIDGEPORT EVENING FARMER, February 13, 1914.

319. *Board of Parole Refuses Pardon to Sophie Kritchman*, THE HARTFORD COURANT, Sept. 4, 1919.

320. *Sophie Kritchman's Pal Applies for Pardon*, THE HARTFORD COURANT, Apr. 21, 1917.

321. *Awaits Gallows, Asks Pardon Board to Let Him Go in Trenches—Carmine Pissniello, Sentenced to Be Hanged, Promises to Give Himself up After War—Other Prisoners Also Ask Chance to Go On Battlefield*, THE HARTFORD COURANT, May 11, 1918.

Sophie's Release and Return to Waterbury

322. *Sophie Kritchman Wants to Go Home after Prison Life*, THE HARTFORD COURANT, July 22, 1919.

323. *Sophie Kritchman Is Out after 11 Years*, THE HARTFORD COURANT, May 9, 1920.

324. *Sophie Kritchman Plans to Marry Naugatuck Man*, THE HARTFORD COURANT, Sept. 27, 1920; *Sophie Kritchman to Be Bride*, THE BRIDGEPORT TELEGRAM, Sept. 28, 1920. *See also* a note in THE BRIDGEPORT TIMES AND EVENING FARMER, Sept. 27, 1920. It seems that Sophie's mother had

also remarried in 1912. *See Mrs. Kritchman Weds*, BRIDGEPORT EVENING FARMER, Apr. 11, 1912.

325. THE HARTFORD COURANT, Oct. 2, 1920.

326. *See* RICHARD H. UNDERWOOD, GASLIGHT LAWYERS (2017).

327. ALLAN McLANE HAMILTON, RECOLLECTIONS OF AN ALIENIST 336 (1916).

328. *Springtime for Sophie Kritchman*, THE HARTFORD COURANT, Oct. 2, 1920.

Mitchell and the Board of Pardons

329. *Mitchell Appeals to State Board for His Freedom*, NAUGATUCK DAILY NEWS, June 13, 1922.

330. *Joseph Mitchell May Be Innocent*, THE HARTFORD COURANT, Sept. 25, 1923.

331. *Joe Mitchell and 7 Others Freed by Pardon Board*, THE BRIDGEPORT TELEGRAM, Dec. 18, 1923.

332. *To Consider Pardon of Joseph Mitchell*, THE HARTFORD COURANT, Dec. 7, 1923.

333. *See also Joe Mitchell Is Granted Pardon*, THE BRIDGEPORT TELEGRAM, Dec.19, 1923; *3 Life Prisoners among 8 Freed by Board of Pardons*, THE HARTFORD COURANT, Dec. 19, 1923.

334. *Joseph Mitchell, Freed from Prison, in Union City Today—He Visited Rev. William J. Fanning at S. Mary's Rectory—Happy as Boy Out of School and Grateful to All His Friends—He Left the Prison Late Yesterday Afternoon and Spent Last Night at Home of Louis M. Raffel in Waterbury—To Raise Fund with Which to Give Mitchell a New Start in Life*, NAUGATUCK DAILY NEWS, Dec. 10, 1913.

335. *Notify Aged Mother of Mitchell's Pardon—Sophie Kritchman Asked Governor to Oppose Release*, THE HARTFORD COURANT, Dec. 20, 1923; *See also, Waterbury Greets "Joe" Mitchell*, Hartford Courant, Dec. 23, 1923.

336. *See Templeton Sends Sympathy Message*, THE HARTFORD COURANT, Jan. 14, 1924.

337. *Attacks on Courts in Mitchell Case Disturbs Judges*, THE HARTFORD COURANT, Jan. 18, 1924.

338. *Id.*

339. *Attack on Courts in Mitchell Case Disturbs Judges—Governor Gets Request Not to Encourage Dangerous Agitation in Name of Pardoned Lifer—Catholic Church Notifies Priests—Fathers Murray and Fanning Receive Word from Ecclesiastical Authorities on Mitchell Case*, THE HARTFORD COURANT, Jan.18, 1924; *Templeton Sends Sympathy Message—Keeps Away from Latest Meeting Held for Paroled Convicts...*, THE HARTFORD COURANT, Jan. 14, 1924.

340. *After Weisman's Scalp*, THE HARTFORD COURANT, Dec. 10, 1922.

341. *See Louis M. Raffel of Waterbury Sued*, THE HARTFORD COURANT, July 26, 1923; *Raffel-Weisman Feud*, THE HARTFORD COURANT, July 29, 1923; *Weisman Libel Suit Thursday—Deputy Sheriff Asks $50,000 Damages from Real Estate Man*, THE HARTFORD COURANT, Mar. 9, 1924; *Raffel Case*, THE HARTFORD COURANT, Mar. 16, 1924; *Testimony in Murder Trial in Raffel Suit*, THE HARTFORD COURANT, Mar. 21, 1924.

342. *See* THE HARTFORD COURANT, Dec. 23, 1923.

343. *See Freed 'Lifer' 'Used' in Feud—Agitation over Jot* [sic] *Mitchell Also Aimed at Hebrew Church Head—Judges Attracted by the Disturbance—Find Row between Realtors at Bottom of Attack on State Court*, THE HARTFORD COURANT, Jan. 19, 1924.

344. *Id. See also Weisman Libel Suit Thursday*, THE HARTFORD COURANT, Mar. 9, 1924; *Raffel Case*, THE HARTFORD COURANT, Mar. 16, 1924; *Testimony in Murder Trial in Raffel Suit*, THE HARTFORD COURANT, Mar. 21, 1924. For other coverage of the libel case, see *Sheriff Reilly Court Witness—In Waterbury Row over Deputy*, THE JOURNAL (Meriden, CT) Mar. 20, 1924; *Weisman-Raffel Suit*, THE HARTFORD COURANT, Mar. 23, 1924; *Weisman Case*, THE HARTFORD COURANT, Mar. 30, 1924; and an untitled note in THE HARTFORD COURANT, Jan. 20, 1924.

345. *Weisman Awarded $3,000 Judgment in Libel*, THE BRIDGEPORT TELEGRAM, Apr. 11, 1924; *Weisman Wins Libel Suit against Raffel*, THE HARTFORD COURANT, Apr. 11, 1924.

Afterword

346. *Out of the Whirlwind*, 171–173.

347. I refer the reader to Model Rule of Professional Conduct 3.3(a)(3).

348. In his day author Walsh was accused of anti-Semitism. For an odd
exchange, see Dr. Cecil Roth, *Jews, Conversos, and the Blood Accusation
in Fifteenth Century Spain,* in the DUBLIN REVIEW, Oct. 1932, at 219-231,
where Dr. Roth is commenting on Walsh's Isabella of Spain (1930). Walsh's
reply to Dr. Roth is at pp. 232-252 of the same issue. I found a number
of passages in *Out of the Whirlwind* to be disturbing. For example, at pp.
251-252, defense lawyer Kelley gives his explanation as to why the "Yankee
farmer" Calvinists on the jury would believe a Jew before they would
believe an Italian or a Lithuanian. He muses, "I don't know why that
should be, unless—well, there has always been a curious affinity between
the Calvinists and the Jews. Their religion was a reversion in some ways
to the Old Testament. And did you ever notice how many hooked noses
there are among these New England Baptists and Methodists? And come
to think of it, it was the Puritans who let the Jews back into England,
wasn't it?" The prolific Walsh was very religious, to say the least. He had
strong views on Jews and Protestants, which one can find in his books
Isabella of Spain (1930), *Phillip II* (1937), and *Our Lady of Fatima* (1947).
Kaplan, something of a hero in the novel, is a Jew, but Walsh's treatment
of him is ambiguous. Walsh was staunchly anti-communist, too, and he
refers to both Stephen West's and Kaplan's sympathy with the Russian
Revolution. Walsh's first book, *The Mirage of the Many* (1910), was a
warning to those who might be seduced by Socialism. For a review of the
book, see *St. Louis Post-Dispatch* (MO), Oct. 22. 1910. ("One might safely
hide a $10 bill in the middle of the volume, confident that of the first
dozen readers, not one would not get far enough to find the money…A
Tasteful binding seems wasted upon this book.") *See also 'The Mirage of
the Many,'—Walsh's Novel Treats of Development of Socialism in 1952,* THE
BOSTON GLOBE, Sept.10, 1910. An excerpt from the review: "Such a crazy
lot of socialists or anarchists, or whatever they are, you never saw. They
just revel in carnage. It is wonderful what men will do when they get
bughouse on economics… It should be read by everyone who has read
Jack London and by everyone who has not." The allusion was to socialist
London's novel *The Iron Heel* (1907), which is, in part, a lament on the
crushing of an early twentieth-century socialist revolution by the *oligarchy*
(a coalition of bankers, industrialists, and politicians). The Soviets made it
into a silent, propaganda movie in 1919. The Bernie Sanders presidential
run in 2016 may have inspired the reappearance of the work as a stage play.
See Geoff Bailey, "Jack London Strides onto the Stage," Aug. 8, 2016, at
https://socialistworker.org/author/geoff-bailey.

According to Bailey, "[R]eaders of Socialist Worker will especially appreciate the scenes of the 1912 election campaign between a Republican supporter of the Iron Heel, Everhard [London's hero] for the socialists, with the Democratic Party caught in between."

349. Perhaps this bit of plot was suggested to Walsh by news articles about a suicide attempt by a John Weisman. *See Drinks Carbolic Acid*, RECORD JOURNAL (Meriden, CT), Aug. 16, 1913; *Sorry He Didn't Take a Fatal Dose—John Weisman of Union City Drinks Carbolic Acid, but May Live*, THE HARTFORD COURANT, Aug.16, 1913; *Weisman of Naugatuck Pleads Bankruptcy—Believed He is the Man Who Attempted Suicide Here Recently*, THE HARTFORD COURANT, Sept. 15, 1913. However, I am sure that this was not the same John Weisman. I found it interesting that a 1924 article in *The Bridgeport Telegram* reported that in that year a despondent man named John Weisman, who had the same name "as that of a prominent local political leader," poisoned himself with iodine, and when the poisoning was first reported, "many people thought that Deputy Sheriff John Weisman was the victim." *See Despondent Man Takes Iodine Dose*, THE BRIDGEPORT TELEGRAM (Bridgeport, CT), Sept. 9, 1924.

350. Kleinfeld, Circuit Judge, in *United States v. Zuno-Arce*, 44 F.3d 1420 (9th Cir. 1995).

351. *See also Joe Mitchell, Free, Weds in Waterbury*, WATERBURY REPUBLICAN, Aug. 9, 1924.

352. *Kritchman Verdict: Sophia Guilty*, WATERBURY REPUBLICAN, Mar. 26, 1910.

353. *Former Congressman William Kennedy Dead*, BRIDGEPORT TIMES AND EVENING FARMER, June 19, 1918.

354. *John Weisman, Waterbury Constable, Dies after Election*, THE HARTFORD COURANT, Oct. 5, 1927; see also a note of the death in BRIDGEPORT TELEGRAM, Oct. 6, 1927.

Acknowledgments

355. From FRANCIS BACON, NOVUM ORGANUM (1620).

Selected Bibliography

Court Records and Official Documents

I. Vol. 103, *Connecticut Supreme Court Records and Briefs*, Third District, January Term (1911), containing the following (409 printed pages):

Indictment
Judgment
Defendant Joseph Mitchell's request for a finding
Findings of Facts (Williams, J.)
State's offer of proof
Defendant, Sophie Kritchman's offer of proof
Rulings during trial
Defendant Joseph Mitchell's requests to charge
Charge to the jury (Williams, J.)
Defendant Joseph Mitchell's application to rectify the appeal
Defendant Joseph Mitchell's appeal
Brief in behalf of Joseph Pecciulis, alia Joseph Mitchell, by Stoddard, Goodhardt & Stoddard, of Counsel
Brief on behalf of appellee (the State), by John Kellogg, Assistant State's Attorney
State v. Kritchman, et al. 79 A. 75 (1911)
State v. Pecciulis (Joseph), 84 Conn. 152, 79 A. 75 (1911)

II. Miscellaneous Records of the Superior Court (Typed and Handwritten)

Objection of Sophis (sic) Kritchman to order for joint trial
Judgment on plea of former jeopardy, Feb. 4, 1910
Plea of former jeopardy and motion for discharge
Replication to plea of former jeopardy, etc., Feb. 14, 1910, relating to letter threatening Sophia Kritchman

Answer to Replication, Feb. 14, 1910
State's Demurer to portions of replication, Feb. 14, 1910
Amendment to Plea of former jeopardy and motion for discharge, Feb. 14, 1910
Memorandum of Decision – denying plea of former jeopardy
Formal objection to the impaneling of the jury
State's Exhibit 9
Defendant Mitchell's requests to charge
Defendant Kritchman's request to charge
Charge given by the court
Judgment
Motion to set aside verdict and for [a] new trial
Sophie Kritchman's notice of appeal
Joseph Pecciulius's notice of appeal
Defendant Joseph Mitchell's request for a finding
*Draft Finding by Joseph Pecculius, alias Joseph Mitchell, containing transcribed
     testimony of Victoria Dalton, and the direct examination of Sophia Kritchman
     by William Kennedy*
*Transcript of continued examination (March 11, 1910) of Sophia Kritchman by
     William Kennedy*
*Selected, transcribed testimony of Patrick J. Monahan, Antonas Kulvinskas, Jon F.
     McGrath, Dr. E. H. Johnson, Thomas Colasanto, and Dr. Nelson A. Pomeroy*
State's draft of counter-finding, including selected testimony
Trial Court's findings (Williams, J.)
*Defendant Joseph Pecciulius', alias Jospeh Mitchell's, application to rectify the
     appeal*
The defendant, Joseph Pecciulius, alias Joseph Mitchell's, appeal
Miscellaneous subpoenas
Letter from Judge Curtis to John P. Kellog

Court Opinions

Ex parte Tommy Washington v. State of Alabama, 562 So. 2d 1304 (Ala. 1990)
Griswold v. Connecticut, 381 U.S. 479 (1965)
Hacker v. Indiana, Court of Appeals Case 19A-CR-1577 (Ind. Ct. App., Jan. 12,
     2021)
State v. Howell, 80 Conn. 668, 69 A. 1057 (1908)
State v. Kritchman et al., 84 Conn. 152, 79 A. 75 (1911)
State v. Pecciulis (Joseph), 84 Conn. 152 (1911)
United States v. Zuno-Arce, 44 F.3d 1420 (9th Cir. 1995)
Williamson v. United States, 512 U.S. 594 (1994)

Special Collections and Archives

Library of Congress
The Mattatuck Historical Society

Books

Bacon, *Novum Organum* (1620)

Bugliosi, *Outrage* (1996)

Davidson, *A Century of Homeopaths; Their Influence on Medicine and Health* (2014)

Federal Rules of Evidence

Garrett, *Convicting the Innocent: Where Criminal Prosecutions Go Wrong* (2011)

Goodheart, *Female Capital Punishment: From the Gallows to Unofficial Abolition in Connecticut* (2020)

Greenburg, *The Mad Bomber of New York: The Extraordinary True Story of the Manhunt That Paralyzed a City* (2011)

Guttmacher and Weihofen, *Psychiatry and the Law* (1952)

Hamilton, *Recollections of an Alienist* (1916)

Hopkins, *Murder Is My Business* (1970)

London, *The Iron Heel* (1907)

Meyers and Walker, *Historic Columbus Crimes* (2010)

Model Rules of Professional Conduct

Pape, *History of Waterbury and the Naugatuck Valley*, Vol. 1 (1918)

Pinta, *The Murder Trials of Harry K. Thaw (1907 and 1908) and Dr. Arthur Waite (1916) and The Perplexing Concept of 'Constitutional Infirmity'*

Reynolds and Murray, *Wicked Waterbury: Madmen & Mayhem in the Brass City* (Kindle) (2008)

Underwood, *Gaslight Lawyers: Criminal Trials & Exploits in Gilded Age New York* (2017).

Underwood, *Crimesong: True Crime Stories from Southern Murder Ballads* (2016)

Walsh, *Out of the Whirlwind* (1935)

Book Chapters and Periodicals

Brooks, "Dying Declarations," Chapter 3.1 in *Fictional Discourse and the Law*, ed. Hans J. Lind (2020)

Hoyt, *The Judge's Power to Comment on the Testimony in His Charge to the Jury*, 11 Marq. L. Rev. 67 (1927)

Roth, *Jews, Conversos, and the Blood Accusation in Fifteenth Century Spain*, Dublin Rev., 219-231 (Oct. 1932)

Underwood, *Mr. Howe's Last Case*, XXXI Legal Stud. F. 801 (2007)

Newspapers

Alexandria Gazette (DC)
The Boston Globe
Bridgeport Evening Farmer (CT)
The Bridgeport Telegram
Bridgeport Times and Evening Farmer
The Brooklyn Citizen
Courier Journal (Louisville, KY)
The Day (New London, CT)
The Hartford Courant
The Journal (Meriden, CT)
Los Angeles Herald
Meriden Morning Record (CT)
The Morning Call (Allentown, PA)
Naugatuck Daily News (CT)
New York Daily News
New York Times
The Norwalk Hour (CT)
Norwich Bulletin (CT)
Ogden Morning Examiner (UT)
Pittsburgh Daily Post
Pittsburgh Post-Gazette
Pittsburgh Press
Record Journal (Meriden, CT)
The Republican American (CT)
The Star (Seattle, WA)
Sun (New York, NY)
St. Louis Post-Dispatch (MO)
Sunday Republican (Waterbury, CT)
Tampa Times (FL)

Waikato Times (Hamilton, NZ)
Waterbury Republican (CT)
Westmoreland Recorder (KS)

Illustration Credits

Numbers refer to illustration numbers in the text and appear courtesy of the following:

Almay Inc.: 5
Author's Private Collection: 4, 12, 24, 26
Connecticut Museum of Culture and History [formerly Connecticut Historical Society]: 25
Library of Congress: 2
Collection of the Mattatuck Museum, Waterbury, Connecticut: 1, 20
Miscellaneous Records of the Superior Court: 13, 23
Naugatuck City Directory (circa 1909): 10
Naugatuck Daily News: 7
The Star (Seattle, WA): 14
Waterbury Republican: 6, 8, 9, 11,15, 16, 17, 18, 19, 21, 22
Wikipedia: 3, 27

A Note About the Cover Art

The portrait (*Sophie*) included in the cover design is based on a black and white photograph in the public domain, 1910 (unknown photographer) of Sophia Kritchman taken during her murder trial. The image appeared in the *Waterbury Republican* on February 4, 1910, and *The Bridgeport Times and Evening Farmer* on March 26, 1910. Annelisa Hermosilla, the cover artist, has reinterpreted the 1910 image in a portrait, using a ballpoint pen to add blue colors and achieve the value contrast (darks and lights). Sketch lines and cross hatches mark proportions and create hair and other physical and costume features to give the art a painterly touch.

Index

Note: Page numbers in italics indicate a figure (photographs, drawings, and documents) and locators containing the letter *n* indicate endnotes

ABOUT THE AUTHOR

Richard H. Underwood, University of Kentucky University Research Professor and Professor Emeritus of Law at the University of Kentucky J. David Rosenberg College of Law, is the author of *Springtime for Sophie: Murder and Madness in a Connecticut Mill Town*, *Gaslight Lawyers: Criminal Trials & Exploits in Gilded Age New York*, and *CrimeSong: True Crime Stories from Southern Murder Ballads*. He is also the co-author of several books on evidence, trial technique and legal ethics. Underwood has published numerous articles on the law, legal history, perjury, famous trials, and true crime. He has lectured or presented papers on diverse subjects at conferences across the United States and in London and Amsterdam.

www.ingramcontent.com/pod-product-compliance
Lightning Source LLC
Chambersburg PA
CBHW052017030426
42335CB00026B/3182